PENNY ARCADE™

9

ONI PRESS

AN ONI PRESS PUBLICATION

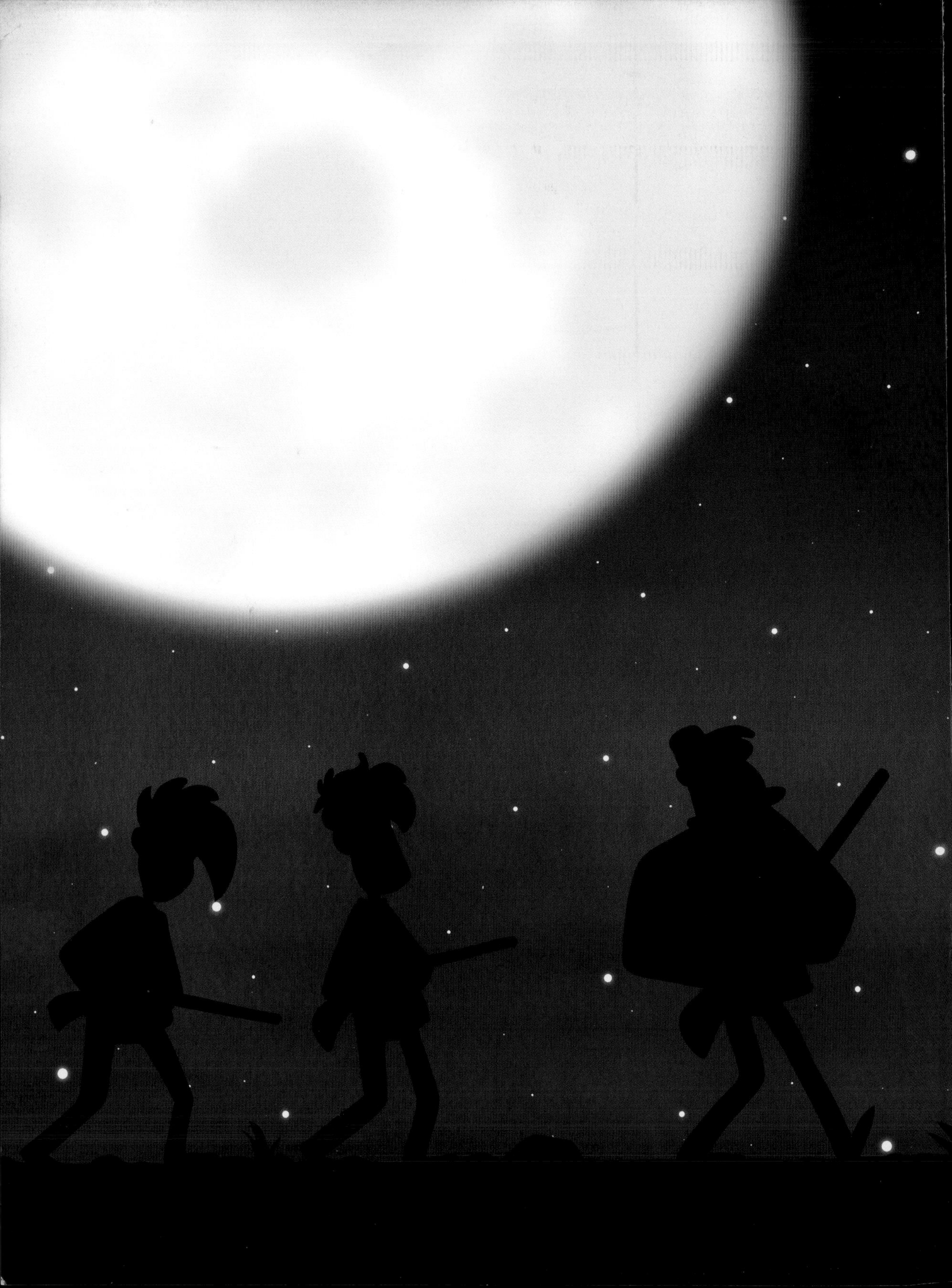

PENNY-ARCADE.COM

BY JERRY HOLKINS & MIKE KRAHULIK

Penny Arcade V9: Passion's Howl
This volume collects comic strips from the Penny Arcade website,
originally published online from January 3, 2008 through December 31, 2008.

Designed by **Troy Look**

Edited by **George Rohac**

Published by Oni Press, Inc.

Joe Nozemack publisher
James Lucas Jones editor in chief
Keith Wood art director
George Rohac director of business development
Tom Shimmin director of sales and marketing
Jill Beaton editor
Charlie Chu editor
Troy Look digital prepress lead
Robin Herrera administrative assistant

ONI PRESS, INC.
1305 SE Martin Luther King Jr. Blvd.
Suite A
Portland, OR 97214
U.S.A.

Become our fan on Facebook: facebook.com/onipress
Follow us on Twitter: @onipress
onipress.tumblr.com
onipress.com
penny-arcade.com

First edition: March 2013
ISBN 978-1-62010-007-3
Library of Congress Control Number: 2012952563

10 9 8 7 6 5 4 3 2 1
PRINTED IN CHINA

Foreword by Stephen Silver

In 1997, Mike and Jerry submitted a comic to *NextGen* magazine. The strip was rejected. So they submitted another. It got rejected, too. They continued to submit strips to *NextGen* until they were asked to stop. But, instead of giving up, Mike and Jerry found another outlet for their comics and now, 15 years later, I am honored to be writing the foreword to their 9th collection of comics and their 10th book. This one includes all of their comics from 2008.

Their story is a great reminder that if we work hard, prepare ourselves, and have our eyes and ears open for opportunity, our dreams can become a reality; that our failures can be stepping-stones to success and not dead ends.

I've had plenty of personal failures and, like many creators, had people tell me that I could "never make a real living as an artist." I chose not to believe them and worked hard to practice my passion until I found success. Mike and Jerry have done the same by remaining dedicated to their work, to their audience, and to the art community. They offer hope to new artists not just by showing us one path to success, but by highlighting the habits of successful artists: perseverance, self-belief and creativity—in composition and expression, and also when solving problems. *Penny Arcade*, to me, is a true inspiration, and a reminder to all of us that as long as we keep going and keep trying we'll eventually succeed in what it is we truly want to do.

I've had a table at San Diego Comic-Con for 15 years where I sell my own self-published art books. I'm always excited to be there and especially to meet fellow artists. One year, I remember a friend coming to me during setup and asking if he could introduce me to Mike. "He is a super huge fan of yours and the *Clerks: The Animated Series* designs. He is creating his own comic." A new fellow artist! Of course I said yes. That was in 2002. Since then I've made a point of stopping by the *Penny Arcade* booth each year and watching it grow. I am so proud and also excited that, three times each week, I get to watch Mike continue to improve himself as an artist before my eyes, knowing that he and Jerry are doing exactly what they want to be doing.

Steve Jobs said it best: "Your time is limited, so don't waste it living someone else's life. Don't be trapped by dogma—which is living with the results of other people's thinking. Don't let the noise of other's opinions drown out your own inner voice. And most important, have the courage to follow your heart and intuition. They somehow already know what you truly want to become. Everything else is secondary." Steve Jobs followed this mantra to success. So did Mike and Jerry when they started publishing their work online. And so can you. You are your own control center, you get to hit the buttons, file the reports and set in motion any orders you wish, you just need the belief and courage to do so. I respect and honor what *Penny Arcade* has brought to the art community. They led the pack in online comics and showed us that we can build an audience by showcasing ourselves at conventions. That we can succeed by being creative and not competitive, with hard work and dedication. I know that there is much more to come from these two, I'm truly looking forward to the fun ahead. Well done, boys!!!!

— *Stephen Silver*
   September 12, 2012

Intro 9

We're really getting into it, now. Before, I would find a comic that I still liked, and it would be a treat! It was like reaching into a pocket and finding a largely intact Werther's Original that only has a *little* bit of lint clinging to it. Now, I don't know. I actually like a lot of these comics. I liked making them. That's not typically how it goes; I couldn't tell you which comics we made last week. I gotta push them out so I can have room for new comics I have to make. I see the motherfuckers in this book, and we bump fists.

We're tight.

This book also has many excerpts from the newspost, which is kind of new. I've dropped them in on occasion before, especially if it was something of an extended nature, but this is the first time I've grabbed great handfuls of stuff and said "I like that" without feeling the need to resort to some kind of ironic dismissal. Recall that for the first several years of the site, I didn't even archive the newsposts: I just deleted that field out of the HTML and started fresh. These days, the posts I do are a Thing. They weren't always.

I would never have done this otherwise, I wouldn't even have known that I could. There is no doubt in my mind that I would have fixed computers all my life and been incredibly unhappy. I am this person only because you gave me an opportunity to be, and I can't thank you enough.

— *Tycho Brahe*
Seattle, WA
September 17, 2012

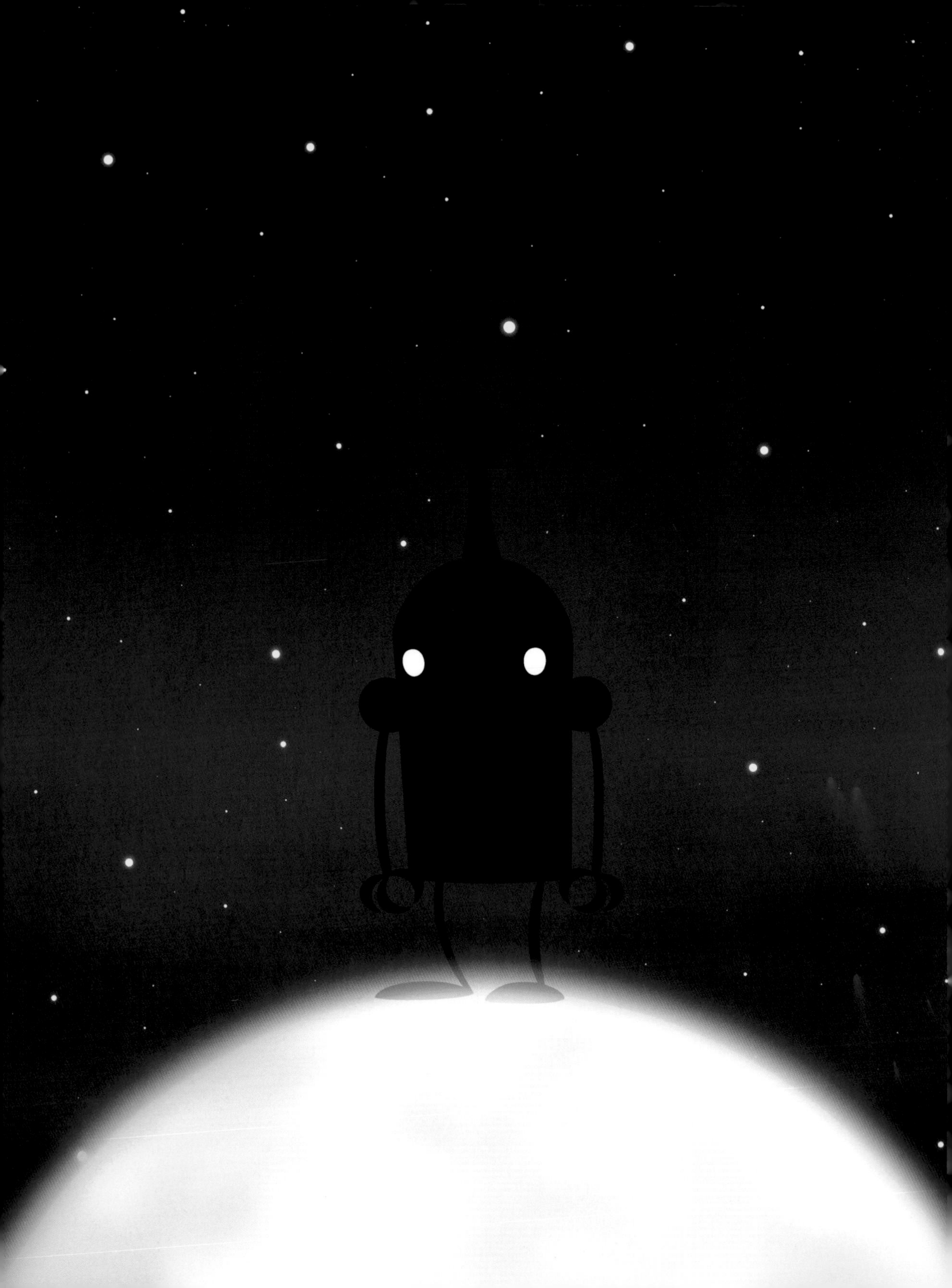

NOT THAT WE MIND

January 04, 2008 Welcome back, and it looks like we're starting off with a weird one. I am always incredibly wary of attempts to manipulate me via merchandise or limited edition whooziwhatsits, for reasons which are explained shortly. I have to be on my shit. So when I opened a box from someone I didn't know full of treasures from EA, my hackles immediately went up, resulting in this strip. The guy lost his job over it. I met him years later; he was really nice.

I talked to him on the phone immediately afterward, though, and the post from that day deals with just how... well, here:

My apology was accepted by the man who sent said DS, and we talked all night on the phone. We are now considering a fall wedding. The first part is true; you may disregard the rest. Or keep the last part, however you want things to play out. We can make this collaborative.

My job, which I usually think of as "uploading jpegs," is tremendously complex sometimes. Let me explain. If someone involved in the promotion of a game sends me a DS that may be used either as a personal gift or as a donation to charity—as was the case here, according to the letter—does the latter negate the former? Or should we determine the propriety of each possibility as discrete moral event? We were talking about a portable game system a minute before, and now all of the sudden we're talking about ethics.

There are people in the games industry whose job it is, literally, to befriend you—and you must constantly correct for it. I don't apologize for this process. If one wishes to write about videogames, they must constantly bat away sucking, vile tendrils. On this topic, you will find wide agreement.

It may be that you don't care about things like this—but I had better care, because I have a responsibility to you. People have been trying to get to *you* through *me* for years. I don't believe this situation falls under that distinction, but even so—I'm uncomfortable with the idea of Child's Play donations coming along with review content through the PR channel. I think it deserves protection from that.

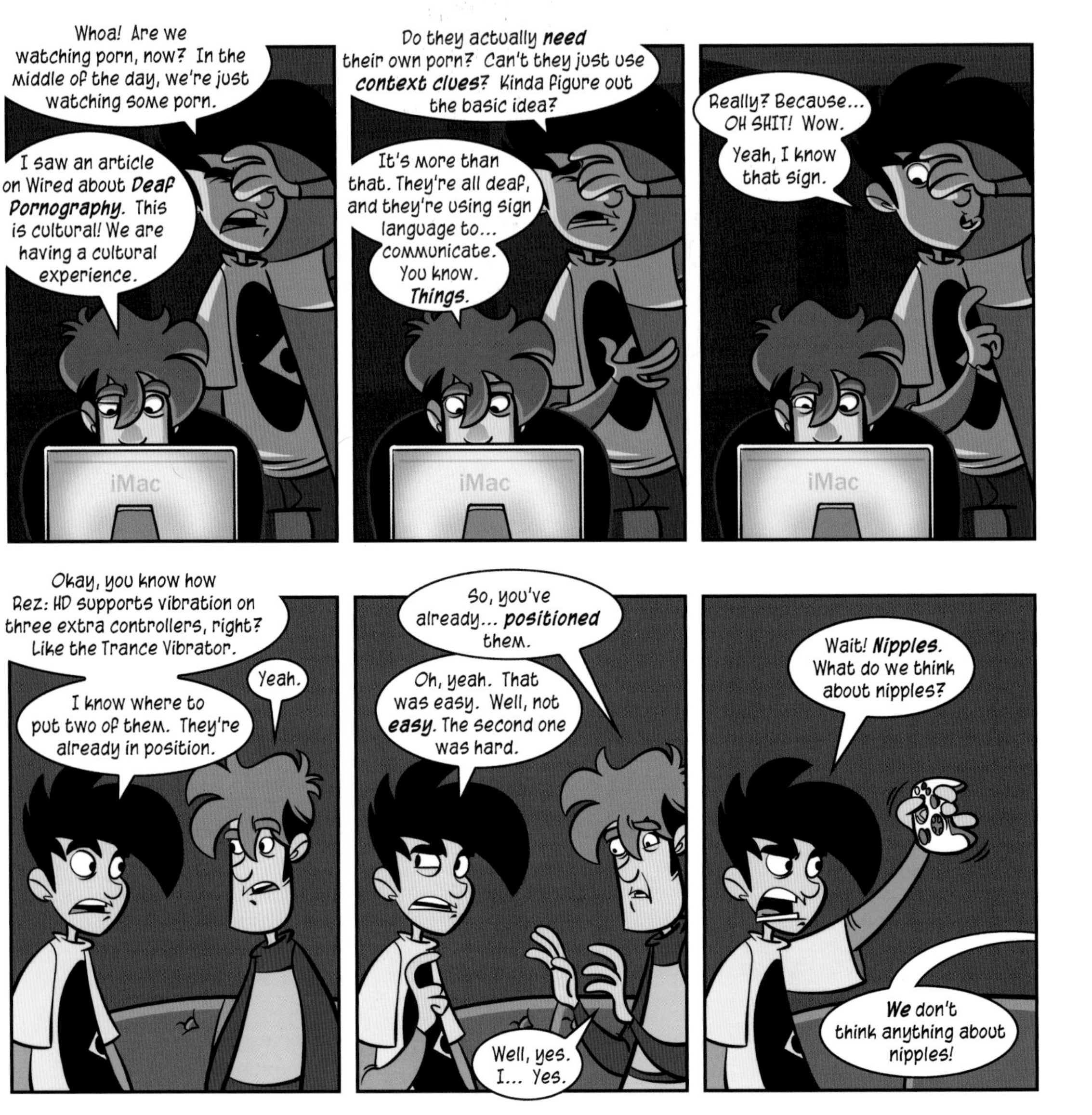
Whoa! Are we watching porn, now? In the middle of the day, we're just watching some porn.
I saw an article on Wired about Deaf Pornography. This is cultural! We are having a cultural experience.
iMac
Do they actually need their own porn? Can't they just use context clues? Kinda figure out the basic idea?
It's more than that. They're all deaf, and they're using sign language to... communicate. You know. Things.
iMac
Really? Because... OH SHIT! Wow.
Yeah, I know that sign.
iMac
Okay, you know how Rez: HD supports vibration on three extra controllers, right? Like the Trance Vibrator.
Yeah.
I know where to put two of them. They're already in position.
So, you've already... positioned them.
Oh, yeah. That was easy. Well, not easy. The second one was hard.
Well, yes. I... Yes.
Wait! Nipples. What do we think about nipples?
We don't think anything about nipples!

UNIVERSAL THEMES

January 7, 2008 I don't know why I was so surprised, really, Rule 34 being what it is. There is no end to all the available, um... configurations. Just as an example, there is porn—and porn in abundance—for Gabe and Tycho. The cartoon ones, not the real ones. THANK GOD. Actually, that might be a good idea for the bonus section in our next book, though I suppose it might change what kind of store you have to buy it in.

SYNESTHESIA, REVISITED

January 9, 2008 Occasionally Gabriel and I will write a strip, and subsequently agree on it, but we both have radically different ideas about what the strip is actually about or what is actually occurring in it. I'll leave you to discern where the confusions were in this case, but it often turns on whether or not we think characters are being literal or figurative in their speech. You'd think we'd be able to discern things like this from, you know, our human language, but apparently not.

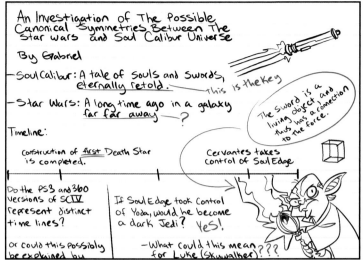

RIGOROUS SCHOLARSHIP

January 11, 2008 From the post: "The urge to create stable frameworks and legitimize our fantasies, to make them internally consistent and therefore *more real* is something we've poked at before. I can't resist it. I always feel the strong compulsion to build upon whatever I enjoy, to understand it better. I can't listen to a song without harmonizing with it, and I can't play a game without imbuing it with sheaves upon sheaves of personally relevant contextual information."

FF2K @ CES2008

January 14, 2008 The Fruit Fucker is but one expression of the overall FuckerCo philosophy, yes, though it's fair to say that these products do share an an overriding "theme."

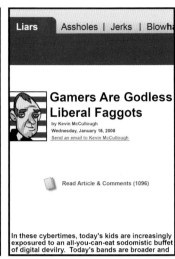

THE STRATAGEM

January 16, 2008 Everything in quotes there is from an actual article that was written by a person, as opposed to an automated script, which is what you would assume given the apparently random word choice. This is a proven tactic now, this nerdbaiting stuff, and it's back in a big way. We are such a reliable source of traffic (and hence, money) that they'd be fools not to pump us for views. These pieces generally take the form of "baldly mercenary theater which purports to be dialogue but is actually just a stranger yelling at you."

WHAT GOES AROUND

January 18, 2008 This is, I have to say, one of the weirder things about our glorious digital future slash present. The entire idea of the Divx player was that you could "watch" a movie you did not entirely "own," made somewhat strange by the fact that you still had this disc in your house that contained the movie. This idea was considered pure madness back then, beyond the pale, but it's almost precisely what the industry settled on for larger scale digital media. I suspect the "owning of digital stuff" conversation will be sticking around for awhile.

ENDLESSLY OCEANIC

January 21, 2008 As gaming (and gamers, for that matter) becomes broader in definition, "digital software experiences" get released that the our ordinary mechanisms of review and our codified approaches to play aren't entirely designed to handle. *Endless Ocean* is exactly what it says on the tin, a big ocean, and you jump off a boat and swim in it. It's really soothing, which is a nutrient I don't normally associate with videogames. Still, people expected a different kind of depth than the one oceans naturally offer. We made this strip to provide, as the post for that day suggested, "a chilling context in which to swim."

THE RECIDIVIST

January 23, 2008 This is a callback to a strip from a previous book, or... the Internet, where I got Gabriel one of those Figure Print things as a present and it ended up becoming a huge problem because his character had "nothing to wear." His videogame character didn't look fancy enough for him to print out. Which I sort of get. A Figure Print Thingy is an opportunity to give your *World of Warcraft* career a physical form. It makes sense that you would want to look your best. In this case, it meant forming an entire guild to "shop" in incredibly dangerous dungeons.

REAL ANSWERS TO PRESSING QUESTIONS

January 25, 2008 Crystallized Demon Blood being the currency of that world, you need lots of it—and it's in every damn thing. We're supposed to be super surprised when a bunch of demons jump out and start going fucking nuts, but when *all objects* are apparently comprised of monster juice that seems to damage the thesis somewhat. I don't know! This shit is practically running out of the taps! Houses in this world are plumbed for hot, cold, and Demon Blood.

A LARGE ROCK AND A STEEP HILL

January 28, 2008 The dialogue has been changed to a certain extent, but the strip is based on a real video promoting their new Stormreach content; you can sort of see the "ch" there in the frame. I had nothing but sympathy for them, but they didn't need it. They were already turning things around internally, shifting the entire experience to a "Free To Play" model the same way they would eventually use with *Lord Of The Rings Online*. Now, "DDO" is going gangbusters, with a new expansion into the Forgotten Realms and everything! I wouldn't have called that.

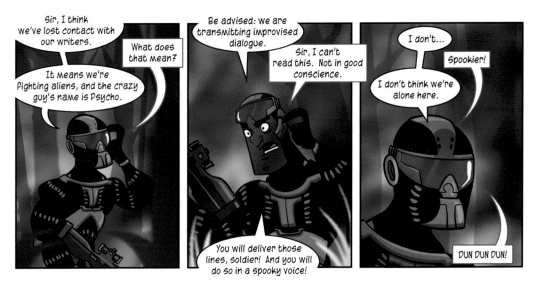

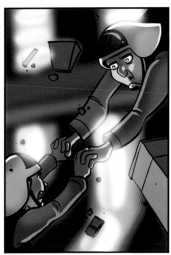

A NARRATIVE IN CRISIS

January 30, 2008 As suggested in that day's post, "The graphics in this game are stupefying. Good graphics will get you about two sentences here, but run at a high resolution, some of these cutscenes cease to be enjoyable and instead become *horrifying*. Once you stop talking about the graphics, the conversation is basically over. *Crysis* is the sequel to *Far Cry*, period. With *Mass Effect*, you had amazing storytelling whose technology never quite held up its end. In *Crysis*, you have precisely the opposite." I should emphasize that merely being the sequel to *Far Cry* is good enough for me; given the surrounding text, that doesn't really come across.

TWO BODIES IN SPACE

February 1, 2008 *The Force Unleashed* has customized simulation technology that does all kinds of weird stuff. You can bend metal, or carbonite, or whatever metal they have in there. You can bend the shit out of it, seriously just bend it for real. Crystal, too! Whatever you want to bend. But when people get flung around they're programmed to grab "grabbable" things in the environment, including other people. So you end up with things that look funny/romantic even then they probably aren't. Maybe I would grab somebody in that situation too, I don't know. I've never been siphoned up into a Force Whorl.

NOAH WEBSTER, YOU'RE MY ONLY HOPE

February 4, 2008 I'm generally thought of as the grammarian around here, and we play it up some-times for the strip—with Mr. Period, for example, and his "Bad Boys of Punctuation"—but I'm only a stickler in comparison to Gabriel. I never know when I have told a person something before, so if you've heard this already, feel free to skip ahead. For me, it's more important to be understood than it is to be correct mechanically. And if trying to express something in a new way harms legibility, I privilege the drive to explore language over clarity or linguistic dogma. Sorry about that; I'm usually very careful not to let people see what I'm actually like.

WE ARE ONLY TRYING TO HELP

February 6, 2008 This middle period was so weird. It really was a comically long install, and it was required, so it was yours to savor. In the post for this strip, I discussed how I don't really associate long installs (or required installs of any kind, really) with my conception of a gaming "appliance." On the other hand, I was amenable to the idea of optional installs. Since then, we've seen various per-mutations of this concept: from Microsoft's optional DVD rips, to downloadable additions that would have once occupied space on the platter, to special upgrades a la *Battlefield 3* that increase fidelity. They're all stopgaps, though. This generation, and its founding principles, are getting long in the tooth.

PHARMACOPSYCHIATRY

February 8, 2008 People have, on many occasions, thanked us for being so frank about anxiety and depression. I gave Mike the customary newspost slot for this strip, because what he was saying seemed like it might help a person. I'll include it here, for the curious:

I've talked a couple times here about my anxiety issues. I've said before that I never thought I could take any kind of medication for it. That's due to the fact that one of the things I was most paranoid about was drugs. It's true that I did finally see a doctor and I have started taking medicine. I felt a little weird about it at first but a friend of mine made a good point. He told me he takes four different pills for his allergies every morning. For some reason that really made sense to me.

So I've always worried about things. I also always knew that most of the time there was nothing to worry about. For me it wasn't even just worrying about something. I understand that everyone worries. The best way I can describe it is "Chain worrying." I'll try and give you an example. The medication I picked up today said it could cause dizziness. That might worry someone for a second and then they would take the pill. For me, though, I had to obsess over it all afternoon. It went something like this: But I drove to work today by myself, will I be able to drive home? What if I can't? How will I know if I can't? Should I call the doctor if I get dizzy? How dizzy is too dizzy? What if the doctor isn't there? Will I need to go to the hospital? Should I get a ride home? I can't leave my car here overnight. The garage closes at 6, what will I do with my car? What if Kara can't come get me? Should I ask Kiko for a ride home? If I get dizzy does that mean it's working? Does that mean it's not working? What if it doesn't work? What if I don't have anxiety disorder, what if I have a worm in my skull that eats brain and shits tumors? To use a term you might be familiar with, my anxiety "stacks."

It was almost impossible to go get help, though, because the very nature of the illness prevents you from getting it. So I worry a lot, I know that. So I start to think, maybe I worry too much. Maybe I have a real problem. Then I think, "no I'm just worrying too much". This is the kind of thing that keeps me awake at night. It's fucking inescapable, like some kind of brain trap. So I have to write off this fear that I might actually be sick as another example of my needless worrying. Add to that the fact that I worry that if I do go to a doctor he'll tell me I have some kind of brain disease, or I'm not treatable, or maybe just as bad that there's nothing wrong with me. All this shit piles up and the result is that I'm 30 and I've never gone to the doctor about it until yesterday.

There were a lot of factors that contributed to me finally going. I've had a friend for a while now who had similar problems. He got help a while ago for it and has been trying to convince me to do the same for more than a year. Also, and this is a big one; I felt like it was getting worse. I had sort of resigned myself to living with it. I had managed it this far, I figured there's no reason I can't keep it up. When I noticed that it was getting worse rather than staying the same I got scared. Not even for myself necessarily but for the people around me. I have a family now and that means I don't have the luxury of indulging my neurosis. I decided that if there really was another way of living, that if I really could get rid of this weight, that I owed it to myself and the people around me to try.

I guess I could experience some sexual side effects but honestly, I was never very good at that to begin with. The increased anxiety is a real concern (hah!) but if it happens at all I'm told it will go away within the first week or so. In the end I'm just crossing my fingers and staying hopeful. It couldn't hurt to try. Unless the medication liquefies my bones. That would hurt.

—Gabe out

Here's what I said in the post immediately after:

He came into work yesterday with a prescription for something that will alter his brain chemistry, which I thought was a big step for the man who refuses to take aspirin. We've long canonized our respective lunacies, believing it is like some artistic sacrament that makes our bizarre endeavor possible. We have *relied* upon them. Or, at any rate, we did.

I thought being crazy was something we did together.

I can remember, even now, how worried I was—that last line really says it all. Everything that has happened here was so improbable, so bizarre, that it didn't seem like something you could modify safely. It is hard to imagine it, but it's all there in the text. There is no question that I resented him for it.

TRAVEL FORM, AND I'M OUT

February 11, 2008 MisterGuy (Like Dudefella before him) is one of Gabriel's go-to handles. But this was something we'd both do, and not simply against "mobs." We played exclusively on PvP servers then, because for every night you spent getting ganked you typically had one where the omnipresent threat of death improved the experience considerably. But, yes. We would often bite off more than we could chew in this regard, and when their friends would come back he or I would be off like a shot. Eventually, he secured some kind of "bird form" which lent the proceedings a bit of novelty.

PROFESSOR LAYTON AND THE PERPETUAL TORMENT

February 13, 2008 I described the Professor Layton series as a "Logic Opera," because the characters you meet break into "puzzle" the way the people in musicals spontaneously break into song. I am a Layton Superfan, though: they're beautiful games, executed beautifully. They're charming as fuck. I also like the task of preparing oneself to perform these spatial feats, and I said as much at the time: "preparing, mentally, a state that is not blank, but clean—like those model garages they have at the home stores. All pegboards and fresh tools and drawers that glide open with no squeak."

THE SPORE CULT

February 15, 2008 Gabriel said time and time again that he could not understand what the Big Deal was about *Spore*, and startled gasps were the inevitable result. You were supposed to like it, because it was a game you were supposed to like; that is the kind of thing he is especially bad at. He doesn't like things for that reason. He likes things because they have a clear and consistent vision. So if you make a game where the player is supposed to supply a non-trivial part of the vision, you're barking up the wrong tree. Or, you aren't barking up his tree. Maybe somebody has a tree like that, but not him.

THE UPDATE

February 18, 2008 And it was an incredible relief. That is the awful thing about anxiety, that it tricks you into thinking that you are just "an anxious person," as opposed to someone with a condition that can be eased. What I considered the capital-C Crazy, the part of him that I work with to make these Goddamn comics, was wholly intact. His bizarre, unique perspective was perhaps informed by a lifetime of anxiety, but it was not synonymous with it. We could get that caustic bullshit pumped out and still be about our dark work. Works, plural. We could be about our dark *works*.

THE AREAS OF OUR EXPERTISE

February 20, 2008 It's the sort of thing you want very much to be true, to have the jumbled troves of knowledge our people amass prepare us for us for some imminent, incredibly elaborate, disturbingly specific scenario. Like any collector of ephemera, driven to hoard it by an unnameable urge, we want to know that our reward for a job rigorously, perhaps even *religiously* attended to is forthcoming. It may not be! But we know what to call something that is part snake, part lion, and part goat, and maybe that's enough.

REQUIEM FOR A RAT

February 22, 2008 One of the core pleasures I have had during my tenure as an Internet Demagogue has been talking to people who play games with *their* friends on *their* couch. It was hard to understand why people were so interested in our inside jokes before I knew that they were doing that: there were a lot more people "inside" than we knew about. Many, many people wrote to agree with me that Pikachu was among the most hated Smash Bros. character choices in existence. The boot you see represented in panel three, the one dispensing justice, is my own.

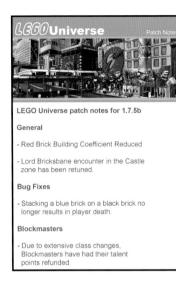

A GLIMPSE INTO THE FUTURE

February 25, 2008 This was long before the game had even come out, long before there was much to know about it, and it was obviously a fair bit before the game met its untimely end about a year and a half into its full release. It was fine; they had (and continue to have) pretty sophisticated tools for the creation of objects with bricks in-game. Trying to follow the thread now, it's not super clear why it *had* to shut down, but money was probably involved in the process. In any case, we couldn't resist approaching it with the level of epic gravity MMO threads always seem to manifest.

THE ALIEN, THE MUTANT, THE HERETIC

February 27, 2008 But the things Cliffy was being excoriated for online simply weren't that freaky. What he said was that people would rather sell four and a half million copies than one million copies, and in a world where the big PC games are *World of Warcraft* and *The Sims*, focusing his efforts on *Gears* was the right play. Maybe that was interesting back then. To give an index of how things can change in unpredictable ways, just before I wrote this paragraph Epic Games announced that its most profitable game ever is *Infinity Blade*—a game for *phones* that you play by rubbing. This shit happens fast.

PREORDER CONFIRMED

February 29, 2008 There's nothing wrong with this rock-solid template for nautical action. Imagine playing as a member of King Q'urub's retinue, the war-wise Black Shells. Imagine dining on a mixed diet of plant and animal matter that included algae, molluscs, and other seafloor detritus! Or, you could be a person on a boat trying to get a crab or whatever. Maybe you want to catch them in your crab-box. There's incredible potential here, and AS USUAL it's being CHOKED OUT by PUBLISHER COWARDICE!

PON PON PATA PON

March 3, 2008 *Patapon* was another "compulsory" game I felt compelled to like. It was charming, certainly. I liked everything about the game that wasn't the game itself; does that make sense? There wasn't enough there for me—there wasn't a way to really play with and around the beat-match stuff. Tapping things to a 4/4 beat made me hungry to add more, and you could sometimes, but other times (like, when it was most important) they'd punish you for it. They made a couple more games after the first one, maybe I should see where the series ended up.

GARY GYGAX
1938 - 2008

ROLLING IN HIS GRAVE

BORDERING ON THE SEMI-TASTEFUL

March 3, 2008 It's no surprise that I am an enthusiast of *Dungeons & Dragons*, and *Vampire*, and other storytelling games besides. This was an opportunity to use the full machinery of the site to honor someone, in our way, which is so exceptionally rare that I couldn't name another time. The post continued the theme, to some measure of success. At least, I think so; maybe you can't run an assessment like that on yourself. Here, you be the judge:

Gygax always struck me as a tremendously sinister name: no mortal name, this. This was the sort of name one earned in the service of horned devils and more primordial shapes of evil, a boon for the loyal servant, placed like a black crown on the bowed head.

The first time I ever played *Dungeons & Dragons*, I was six years old—books with great red demons on the cover that dared us to claim their riches, subtitled by this alien name *Gygax*. My mother was furious when she found my uncles had exposed me to those subterranean burrows, spilling over with rubies, and tourmalines, and the wealth of old kings even songs no longer remember. As a young man, I began hiding the books I bought inside my bed, which had a vast hollow space I had hidden in as a child. These books were soon discovered, and blamed for everything from recent colds to the dissolution of my parents' marriage. I took the wrong lesson, I'm afraid: I didn't learn to fear them. What I learned was that books, some books, were *swollen* with power—and this power projected into the physical realm. Some books contain the machinery required to create and sustain universes.

I owe a tremendous debt to his legacy. I couldn't even calculate how deep.

OUR CRUCIAL PAMPHLET

March 7 , 2008 *Army of Two* was an odd duck. You got the impression from playing it that it had been many games over the course of its life, and what shipped on the disc itself was the limbs and flesh of these disparate products baked into a pie. The tone was especially bizarre, I thought; a parody of masculinity made by people who had only seen men through binoculars. Maybe that's not true at all; maybe it just felt that way. Maybe they delivered exactly what they intended to. If so, these people are exceedingly strange. I'm one to talk, I guess. Take a look through my book here, and tell me if I am of sound mind.

DONGS ARE EVERYWHERE

March 10, 2008 It's a peepee, essentially. He's walking around on some kind of three-dimensional weenis, and it's something he likes slash is interested in. The game is *Echochrome*, you might remember it. The official message at the time was that this was a design for the ages; *Tetris*, specifically, was mentioned. This is something you probably shouldn't do. Talk about your game in *Tetris* terms, I mean. You don't get to determine if your game is a *Tetris* level achievement. That is something all the people out here get to decide.

THE CASE OF TEXAS VS. KRYOLORD

March 12, 2008 Completely true story. Well, not in absolute terms. That's a cartoon, and people don't actually look like that. The chin on this judge is fucking crazy. But "Rockwall District Attorney Ray Sumrow" really did build this beast under false pretenses. The computer is the funny part; the airline tickets for his girlfriend are less funny, and thus did not make the strip. He was sentenced to fifteen years, and was out in twenty months on parole. The standout quote from the story was from FBI Senior Forensic Examiner Gregg, who says he "would not configure a backup computer in that way."

RIVETING

March 14, 2008 To have a young person invest their Wish in you is a profound honor, and it was hard to imagine how we could be worthy of it. Nathan was a good kid, and he was in great spirits; we tried to give him the best day we could. We heard that he lost his fight with cancer a couple weeks ago, friends of his had gotten in touch. Generally speaking, I don't believe in a heaven. But I will make an exception in his case.

THE OMNIPRESENT CORPSE ISSUE

March 17, 2008 I still go back and look at the post for this day from time to time; it came out really strange. I had a super bad rat problem at that point, you might have read about it in another book, and apparently I needed to write about it as therapy or something. Here, look:

Gabriel apparently has a tiny boarder, a friendly creature with tidy fur content to dwell out in the garage. That certainly wasn't *my* experience with the genus, a tattered pageant of misery whose psychic reverberations are still being felt. I recall with unrelenting clarity the beast we secured in a humane trap, rolling and sucking air in its madness, placed on the table in a mockery of polite dinner. It had a musky, unhallowed scent like some primeval mustard, its yellow teeth so long that it could not close its own mouth. Threading its ten fine fingers around the bars, it cried out "We crawl, we swim! We nest and gnaw! We are WE, AND WE DEVOUR!"

I ran then, out of the house, turning in time to see that the entire structure—every stick of it— had been rats all along, rats piled atop one another in such a way as to *suggest* a house. The not-house boiled, exploding, a grey-brown wake of slopping pus and disease.

In any case, Gabriel's pygmy gentleman has chewed one end of one shoelace, and now he must be obliterated. Let this be a lesson to those of you who had been considering a trip out here to nibble on Gabriel's footwear. It is apparently a *death sentence*.

BEDROCK CONCEPTS

March 19, 2008 You would think that, being "dads" or whatever, it might dissuade us from this kind of thing in our strip. By "thing," obviously, I mean baby killing. To understand why this didn't happen, you are welcome to believe that we are monsters. That isn't it, though; the reality is that you have been party to a kind of radical therapy, where two incredibly terrified and neurotic people joke about terrible things not because those things *aren't* terrible but precisely because they are. You are seeing an attempt to inoculate our minds from fear.

THE CREVICE

March 21, 2008 I had forgotten that the Deep Crow was correlated in any way with this rat problem. But this is, what—three or four strips about this tiny creature? That's pretty high profile, more coverage than we give, maybe, ninety percent of topics, but if you've ever had something wrong with a house you understand how much mental "space" it takes up. We had a leak in our house that drip, drip, dripped in my mind for years. You associate yourself with it to a tremendous degree; it maps itself onto your own body. Its sickness is your sickness.

COLD CALLING

March 24, 2008 In defense of Travis, now, it should be said that he's a middle school math teacher. He's not just, like, doing math by himself in the basement or some shit. Math Night is wholly legitimate as an activity. This was back when I was running "Raid Decks" for the *World of Warcraft TCG*, an experience that ended up playing out something like some wild, alternate universe version of *Dungeons & Dragons*. Eventually they dropped the pretense altogether and started roleplaying in earnest. That campaign went on for years, and still occasionally rumbles to life.

A PREVIEW

March 26, 2008 Even though most of it is cut off there in the first panel, I did have to write the whole description field for him to incorporate. I like the air of mystery provided by the truncation, but if you were curious, it reads "Penetrate your enemies with this unbelievable arsenal! This bundle includes The Molester, Sun Cannon, Wrathwave Generator, and the Killwhip. GUARANTEED TO TEAR UP THEIR BACK DOOR!" So, I guess, make other plans vis á vis your back door. I think that's the takeaway, really. Set up a perimeter.

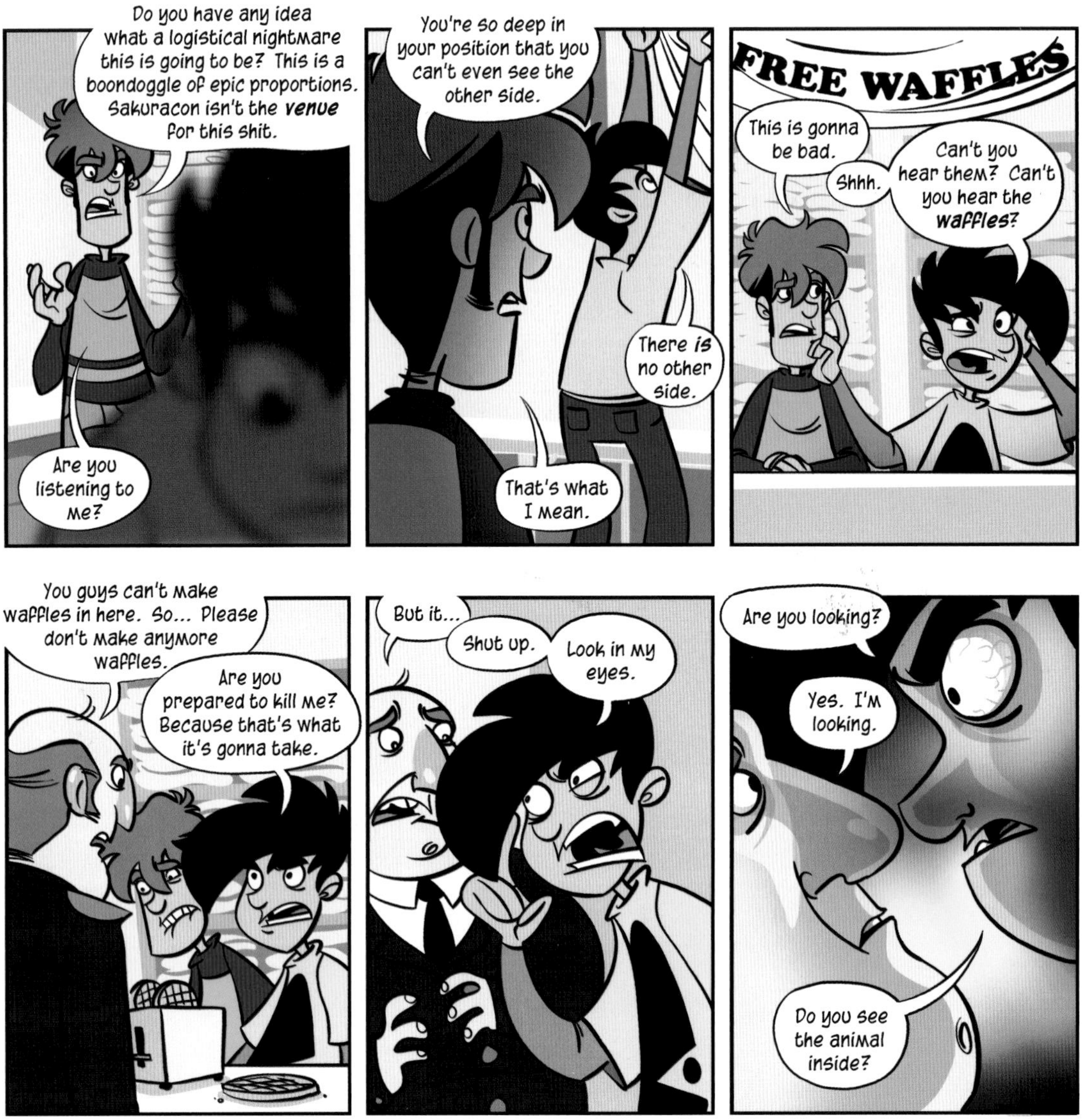
Do you have any idea what a logistical nightmare this is going to be? This is a boondoggle of epic proportions. Sakuracon isn't the **venue** for this shit.
Are you listening to me?
You're so deep in your position that you can't even see the other side.
There **is** no other side.
That's what I mean.
FREE WAFFLES
This is gonna be bad.
Shhh.
Can't you hear them? Can't you hear the **waffles?**
You guys can't make waffles in here. So... Please don't make anymore waffles.
Are you prepared to kill me? Because that's what it's gonna take.
But it...
Shut up.
Look in my eyes.
Are you looking?
Yes. I'm looking.
Do you see the animal inside?

UNCOMPROMISING VISION

March 28, 2008 It occurs to me that I could probably save myself a lot of time by telling you when something *isn't* true. But yes, we toasted eggo waffles, scooped chocolate ice cream on top, and served them from our booth. Not, like for money. They were free. We just thought it would be awesome. Robert came up with an instrument to describe the rate of the waffles we were giving out: WPH, or waffles per hour. At the height, we reached 257 WPH.

A VISION COMPROMISED

March 31, 2008 It's possible I've told this story before, but it's instructional: when I worked as a dishwasher, I used to bring fold-out lawnchairs, sunglasses, and a reggae-stocked beatbox into the pit with me. The manager would poke his head in, open his mouth, close it, then walk away. In my experience, if you're doing something really weird—not dangerous, or threatening, or creepy, just weird—people don't really know how to bin it. At Sakura-Con, the guard couldn't believe what he was asking us not to do. He said it as though the words tasted strange.

NESTED IRONIES

April 2, 2008 I don't know if it's still common, but this "peacebonding" shit was a thing when we were still going to Anime cons. I should see if it is still a thing that happens. Anyway, it never made a lot of sense to me, and it tends to have a net negative impact on people's awesome costumes, which are the primary draw of these conventions anyhow. It's all well and good to have a meticulously detailed, super-reverent persona you've handmade when somebody can festoon with pink ribbons your swords which are not swords and your guns which are not guns.

CLOAKED IN TWILIGHT

April 4, 2008 Oh, wow. Yes, this is what I was talking about before. Good God, those were some late nights. We were still learning what were essentially two games then: the basic *World of Warcraft Card Game*, and then these Raid Decks that had piles of custom rules and cards that appear nowhere else in the game. I got it eventually, and I was able to really grind them down. Then, they'd come back the next week with their decks rebuilt specifically to manage last week's challenges. There are a few different Raid Decks by now; we still break them out every now and again.

HOT DOGS

April 7, 2008 I feel like it's vital to emphasize that I have this cape FOR REAL. For really real! Brenna made it for me, and I've even worn it while adjudicating rounds of this very game. It's all crushed velvet, I think, or velour? I have to be honest when I say that I don't understand the differences *or* the similarities between these two materials! I can fix it, though: I have the Internet. Let's see. Ah, that explains it. Velour is woven, the same way velvet is. It's "two sets of warps and wefts woven at the same time, with additional threads that will become the nap in between." Thanks, Wikipedia! Now I just have to look up "warp," "weft," and "nap."

THE OBLITERATOR

April 9, 2008 The first panel, with its cards flipping around everywhere, is a reference to something you actually do with one of these Boss Decks. Being Boss Decks, after all, they often contain completely huge custom cards. One of these attacks has you dropping the card from a set height over the table, and any card it touches is destroyed. At least, in my memory. To add an element of physicality into this game that is incredibly abstract was really interesting. Plus they never remembered I could do it, so I always got a good haul. The second panel, with its mysterious card and its horrified player, also fills me with icy joy.

HE WHO FIGHTS WITH NERDS

April 11, 2008 I can't really say it enough. Or, maybe I can, but I'm going to say it anyway. It's a strip like this that gives you a keyframe of the site, revealing the passage of time. This was about ten years into the project, and that's how long it took him to develop a deep, true curiosity about these other types of systems. If you've read the other books, or been a long-time reader, you know it was a long time coming. It was this experience—this card experience, specifically—that led to him jumping off the cliff sans parachute. Now he's designing his own tabletop roleplaying system, for crying out loud. And you've seen every step.

WE ARE LIVING IN A MATERIA WORLD

April 14, 2008 When you like a game a lot, or maybe when we do, it makes other parts of our task more difficult. A comic where a JRPG protagonist broods about some shit has probably been done, and we liked *Crisis Core: Final Fantasy VII* so much that all we wanted to do was "research" it. Gabe had one of the "new" PSPs that you could output to a television, so we spent tons of time combining materia and earning XP. If you are a *Final Fantasy VII* nerd, and many people are, it dovetails very nicely into the seventh game. But comics must be made! And this is the comic that happened to get made this particular time.

EXERTIONES

April 16, 2008 This is certainly my problem. I go to the gym twice a week, I have an honest to good-ness trainer and shit, but instead of losing those unwanted pounds I take it as a license to suck down hooch while frying and subsequently eating whole turkeys. This is, no doubt, an example of how one goes about "doin it rong." I need the movement pretty bad, I can feel myself physically sinking into the Earth without it, but I don't really have overarching fitness goals beyond keeping the Crisco circulating in my arteries.

CONTESTED

April 18, 2008 No doubt as a result of our Raid Deck adventures, we had plenty of what are called "Prize Cards" from the *World of Warcraft* card game. These cards could be played like any other, but in addition they had a code on them you could redeem to your actual WoW account. People went batshit for these things, so we thought they would be really cool rewards in a contest of some kind. Then, we had to come up with contest. We decided that "ten word short stories" would be a lot of fun, and then one of the contestants suggested we illustrate the winners. That seemed like a good idea.

THOROUGHLY SCIENTIFIC

April 21, 2008 Pokemon Mystery Dungeon games are not "real" Pokemon games, they don't really stick for us, but they do have other useful technology that can improve lives by determining what kind of Pokemon you might be. Gabriel's "joke" inside the book—that's it's completely eldritch, Lovecraft mythos script—was something I never caught the first time around. Gabe's big face is very big, and demands to be looked at.

LE TWITTRE

April 23, 2008 My relationship with Twitter was very complicated initially, I didn't really know how much I wanted to be a Twitter-er. I stopped doing it for a while. Check the post for that day, if you like. Apparently I was very conflicted indeed.

Readers asked that Gabriel construct a Twitter to let them know when he was starting up a new broadcast, and in the course of this he was exposed to the sort of thing that Twitter is often used for: identifying which *condiment* you have recently applied. We considered a universe where my co-hort was addicted to Twitter's method of consciousness collection, and were horrified by the result.

I can't keep up with things like Twitter or Facebook for some reason. I know that I would hate gardening, and so I don't begin one, and I think there's a similar force at work here. It could constitute the creation, by me, of a system—a *dependent* system. I know for a fact that I will only devote myself to it long enough to disappoint people when I quit. That's why I never announced it when I started using Twitter, and I'm glad, because I've stopped already. I just installed Twitterific, a perfect expression of the service, and the gardening analogy holds. It's all the precision instruments that line the home and garden aisle compressed into a single coordinate: beautiful tools to manage someone else's life.

It's not that I don't get it. I do. I didn't understand the allure until I truly grasped what Twitter's deep intimacy with SMS allowed—a universally available thought machine, my own Ixian dictatel. And this with a built-in editor, a hundred and forty character cage to excise my worst propensities. I tried to include them there, in that very sentence: unnecessary poetry and an addiction to ver-biage. A need to analyze my own writing, *in* writing, *while* I am writing it, makes up the third sin.

I may also have a problem with italics.

The last "tweet" I ever did really explains it all, for me. I was up in Vancouver, and I put up a message saying so, and what kinds of activities I was engaged in. After I did it, I heard a voice—my own voice—saying, "Who the fuck do you think you are? Who are you that you can force your Goddamned minutia on other people, your stupid bullshit, your stone-ground artisanal condi-ments? How dare you. You should be ashamed." And I was.

DISINCENTIVES

April 25, 2008 In no other competition would such a device be tolerated, but there you have it. Gabriel is very good at Mario Kart, and thus hates the Blue Shell. I am less good, and relish it as a result. I wouldn't ever win against him otherwise! I need that fucking thing. I understand why he doesn't like it though—I described it as a "socialist undercurrent that grinds winners and losers together into a smooth paste." The rage he feels when I bean him with it right before sailing over the finish line is savory, almost smoky, and altogether delicious.

LIFE STRATEGIES

April 28, 2008 This is still a problem; I talk about it all the time. The problem is actually two-fold. The first is that there's so much to do in games of that type that it's easy to get "hypmotized" by every little twinkle on the minimap, drawn hither and yon, until you have played for an entire night and you don't really have anything to show for it. I can do that for a while, but I want progress eventually, but *then* I don't feel like I'm getting the most I could out of the genre! Second, games which are broad are rarely deep. It's not a rule, but it's very difficult to pull off. Ultimately, these two things conspire in the game's exile.

MINUTIA

April 30, 2008 I sometimes wonder if he's just testing me with this shit, or if there is some complex latticework of logical mechanisms behind all of it that I can't perceive. That's my experience of it, anyhow: there is a vague sense that some vast, clockwork monolith is clonking in a barely audible juxtaposed dimension, and it is hooked into him somehow.

MAKING AN IMPRESSION

May 2, 2008 Open World Games almost necessarily take liberties, even when they're purporting to give it to you live on the mean-ass streets. The idea that games like Grand Theft Auto take place in a world anything like ours is beyond ridiculous. Even at their most serious, their most grave, they still exist in a place where you stole a semi to get where you were going, carving a valley through a mountain of human corpses on the way. People will forgive the occasional attempt to kill them. Time is nonsense. And, you know, if I'm being completely honest... that's exactly what I like.

THE EXPECTED RESULT

May 5, 2008 You would think that the sequel to *Boom Blox* would be called *"Boom Blox 2,"* it has a certain something, but it is not called that. It is (inexplicably) called *"Boom Blox Bash Party."* Even with this grisly failing made so terrible and plain, these games are must, must, must haves. There are so many discrete "games" on these discs that the value per dollar is off the fucking charts. It's one of the most satisfying examples of raw "play" in recent memory, but apparently sales never indicated taking the series any further. It's criminal, but that's the gruesome lesson of a saturated marketplace: merely being "excellent" is insufficient.

KIDS TODAY

May 7, 2008 I said in the post, and I will tell you now with some measure of shame just how wrong I had some of the particulars. I had "Sex Ed," like everybody else—or, at least, everybody else whose parents were comfortable signing the waiver—and I still had some serious blind spots that wouldn't be rectified until such time as A Wild Vagina approached. I could maintain the Pokemon metaphor, but I won't. I really, really could, though. Like, for hours. As a coming of age metaphor, "Pokémon" is startlingly robust.

DESPERATE MEASURES

May 9, 2008 The same day this comic was posted EA chose to use a less invasive version of the SecuROM product, which has tiers of protection ranging from "Abrasive" all the way up to "Penetrant," which deploys an array of burrowing, subdermal "Compliance Burrs" that sleep just beneath the skin. I would never say that their act was as a direct result of our comic. The comic was, itself, part of a larger conversation that people who play games are always having, all the time. That's what we're doing at our best, anyway. Although occasionally we do focus the prime real estate of the comic on poop, butts, or both.

JE PARLE UN PEU

May 12, 2008 I've talked a little bit about how Gabriel ended up on anti-anxiety medication—Lexapro specifically, though there are certainly others. One of the primary catalysts, aside from unrelenting mental anguish of a kind he still refuses to talk about, was that he wanted to do something remarkable for Kara's birthday. The plan was to take her to France, of all places, but he would freeze up whenever he opened up the airline's *website*. Bolstered chemically, he put it together. That's some Grade A courtin' right there. Nobody ever takes *me* to France.

THE LITTLEST VIGILANTE

May 14, 2008 I was trying to figure out what Comic Convention it was that we would have been able to see this Coolest Thing at, because the year is sorta mapped out for us now and I didn't know which one fit in there. That's when I remembered that there was no PAX East back then, which would ordinarily have loomed large. The show being referred to here, and now I can see it quite plainly in my mind, is the Emerald City Comicon which takes place in the same building as PAX. We miss Sakura-Con now, too, which is sad; I got a lot of shopping done at that show. It was a very expensive weekend.

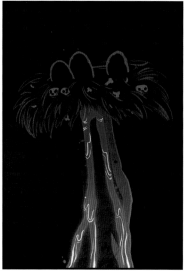

THE FANGSPIRE, PART ONE

May 16, 2008 Whenever we have a small thing, I always have the urge to turn it into a large one. That's the basic version of my problem. Not everything is well-suited to expansion, which I typically learn during the process, but I love this weird bird and this guy who knows way, way too much for some unexplained reason. His cadence is fun to write, certainly. All the great fantasy heroes are, at the root level, exterminators. It gets dressed up fancy, but that's what they do and that's what they are. I liked the idea that there was a line that travelled backward from today's domesticated profession.

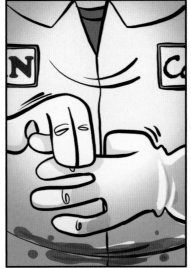

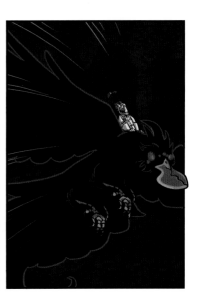

THE FANGSPIRE, PART TWO

May 19, 2008 I had to do this mysterious thumb trick many times while Gabriel was learning to draw it. This is not something people can just draw, it turns out, for the same reason it is strange to look at. It doesn't compute at some level. So, I had to do this trick over and over. You would think that, having been in the service of warlocks and sorceresses or whatever, maybe this weird bird wouldn't be ensorcelled by this kind of Magic 101 type shit, but no. No! That Deep Crow is seriously like "WHAT IN THE ACTUAL FUCKING *FUCK*."

THE FANGSPIRE, PART THREE

May 21, 2008 It is no doubt correlated with my eighties upbringing, but it's written into my very spirit at some level that—under optimal circumstances—every adventure should culminate atop some unlikely beast.

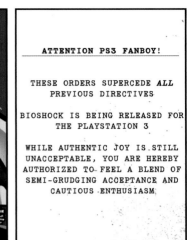

SUPER ULTRA DOUBLE SECRET

May 23, 2008 I could never get the hang of the console wars, partly because I never really saw it as "my fight." I had "consoles" as a boy, but they weren't the same ones Gabriel had. The Magnavox Odyssey² was big in my house, as was the ColecoVision; we never owned an Intellivision, but I certainly coveted their plastic controller inserts and their official *Advanced Dungeons & Dragons* games. But the speed with which people seemed to have their opinions synchronized on issues relating to their console of choice has always impressed me. I was curious as to the precise vector.

THE UNHORSE

May 26, 2008 He has a ton of these cards, I don't know if they were purchased ironically or what, but he's got 'em. He even had a little *Bella Sara* flipbook to store cards *in*. He puts his *Warmachine* cards in there now, cards with big monsters and witches and weirdos who explode when spells come out, but the cover is all horses and rainbows.

Somehow, it's even more intimidating.

APPREHENSION

May 28, 2008 Brenna is fairly serious business when it comes to her *Lord of the Rings* shit, and even as a being situated firmly outside of our conclave of nerd obsession she felt that the movies (while enjoyable) played "fast and loose" and maybe some of that rubbed off on me. Of course, the scenario represented in this strip is no longer the latest thing to be worried about. The thing to be worried about now is that they're making three full films out of one book. Which seems like a lot, but honestly, if you wanna do it right...

MARKET SAVVY

May 30, 2008 I find smoking really confusing. Brenna smoked for awhile, maybe six years or so, and found it almost impossible to quit. That was the only time I would have ever considered her anything like a traditional gamer: *The Sims* was the only thing addictive enough to fill in for that chemical, and she traded one for the other over a period of about a month. When she smells them now, even like eight years later, she wants to start smoking again right away. I had one cigarette almost twenty years ago, and could not understand the allure. Maybe I was doing it wrong.

LITERATURE

June 2, 2008 You say that like it's a *bad* thing, Complete Stranger who is Never Seen In The Comic Again. This series is nuts, though. In book fifteen, "Anita also leaves her former allies, the werelions, to potential death. At a point where Anita and many of her other allies were injured, she asks to have sex with the werelion Rex Joseph so that she could gain the power to heal without the Munin. The Rex refused because he is married and values being faithful to his wife. Also, there were rumors spread about Anita by the lions she refused because they weren't powerful enough for her inner lion."

DON'T DELAY

June 4, 2008 *Ninja Gaiden II* was coming out when we did this comic, but I don't remember if I played it or not. The problem they had is that *Ninja Gaiden* (or the remakes, I guess—Ninja Gaidens *Black* and/or *Sigma*) is more or less perfect. I mean, it's hard, certainly. But it's hard to beat, not hard to play. There are lots of action games I have enjoyed: I like them when they get a little mashy, but also make space to reward precision. *Ninja Gaiden* was the exception that proved the rule, a no-slop, precision ninja simulator. I didn't play *Ninja Gaiden III*, either. It's possible I missed out, but I'm very confident that I played the right one.

ONE POSSIBLE EXPLANATION

June 6, 2008 We wanted to submit an explanation for Jack Thompson's increasingly bizarre behavior—a robust framework, one that fit all the facts. I think we got pretty close. His license to practice law was ultimately revoked as a result of his "unprofessional conduct" which deprived us of a lot of entertainment. Seriously, though. This isn't the outcome you want for a hated foe, a kind of disintegration; a fading out. You don't want them to go out like some street-corner whackjob, denied and disbarred by their peers! It calls your *incredible victory* over them into question!

COUCH DIPLOMACY

June 9, 2008 We got super hooked on a mode we discovered deep, deep in one of the *Boom Blox* menus. There are a ridiculous number of gametypes in this thing, and we knew that from experience, but even we were surprised to find a brilliant kind of four player Battle Jenga thing in there. It was, frankly, beyond: each player has a big castle, all their own, and they each get a turn to hurl ordnance at other people's castles. Each player has a certain number of precious Gems, and once those gems are destroyed, they're out—but when you break somebody's gems, they get more shots. This motherfucker ate up a lot of time.

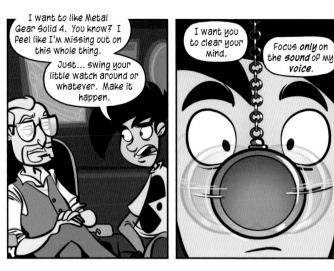

WHOOPS

June 11, 2008 I always buy them, and I always play them, but I rarely feel like I understand a given *Metal Gear Solid*. I really do want to, it's not for lack of trying, and I've invested a tidy sum by now in the prosecution of this goal. I'm usually enjoying them just fine, and then all of the sudden I'll meet a character that makes no fucking sense right alongside some crazy interesting, insightful commentary and get seriously confused. The ones I liked the most were the super, super awesome *Metal Gear AC!D* games, but that might have *something* to do with the fact that they aren't *Metal Gear* games at all, and are instead turn-based(!) collectible card games(!!!).

ON PERSPECTIVE

June 13, 2008 It's hard to imagine this kind of thing now, in Earth's Golden Age, but in a more primitive era people got their knickers in an authentic twist over this kind of thing. At the time, we felt as though Mr. Period (with or without his Bad Boys Of Punctuation) could help us manage some of the gruesome innumeracy on display. Scores aren't especially helpful when it comes to games, for all kinds of reasons—they're used to warp compensation, for one. Oh! And also, they don't really mean anything. There's that. But they also fuel this kind of nonsense, when we could be talking about the actual game.

GRACE IN DEFEAT

June 16, 2008 When playing card games of the collectible variety, particularly in the age of the omniscient Internet, it can get homogenized very quickly. The global tournament infrastructure and the ease with which one can make precision purchases of individual cards means that bringing an armed nuclear warhead to a knife fight is not especially uncommon. At Darkmoon Faire, an organized play event for the *WoW TCG*, we got an instruction in the state of the art where that game was concerned, and it was terrifying. We saw three cards that, when used in tandem, created precisely the effect in the comic. The first panel is a literal transcription.

THE FLAVOR FACTOR

June 18, 2008 The best part of *Spore* was creating monsters. At least, it was to me. My son was a good age for that part, and I still have a few screens I took of these custom mutants—"Mr. Water Creature" and "Doctor Moist" both figure prominently in these digital shots. We never wanted to play with them afterward, we just wanted to obliterate them and then gin up another homemade terror, always with an eye toward maximizing the "frond factor." He was still very young, too young to understand the value of a good frond. That's something I've done my best to instill in him.

THE GABRIEL METHOD

June 20, 2008 I love this comic, but not every mortal craves the last panel, which they suspect may be too "on the nose." It's a common problem, if you are engaged in this kind of writing—that is to say, writing which is ostensibly "humorous"—that people may not like it. I don't have a lot of time to lament it, because between *Penny Arcade* and *Trenches* I am writing new strips more often than not. I'll have another opportunity to impress you in short order, maybe even the next day! But there's an especially dangerous play, called "so bad it's good," which often just gets read as regular old bad.

WHERE THERE IS NO LIGHT

June 23, 2008 My mom wants me to tell you that this is not a game that we ever played, or a thing that ever really happened. Our relationship was complex: she felt strongly that there was a God, indeed, a very specific one, and it was super important to him for some reason whether or not I was touching my peepee at any given time. I needed to believe this also. I was good at believing it, though, so good in fact that I made *other* people believe it. She raised me to be a husband to some alternate universe version of herself. So, she and I had a complex relationship. But she never locked me in a basement.

PAINT THE LINE 2

In 1978, as the specter of nuclear war loomed worldwide,
the UN Security Council introduced Resolution 501.
Known as the Table-Tennis Accords, it decreed that all conflict
between nations be resolved through the dialect of Ping-Pong.

When Chinese terrorists struck down the US Table Tennis Team
in 1979, a rag-tag band of students was forced to play
in their stead. Lead by rivals Johnathan Gabriel and
Tycho Brahe, they were victorious—but not unharmed.

Now, in 1984, the Russian Bear has begun to stir.
In times like these, America needs men whose grip is sure.
Men who play the entire table.

MEN WHO CAN

PAINT THE LINE, PART ONE

June 25, 2008 Whoa, *Paint the Line* is in this book? I have to admit, I'm always a little surprised when we go through the archive like this; that probably comes across. My relationship to these things is much more abstract than you would think, being one of the people who makes them. But, no. In my mind, they're all in a big pile. There's no order to any of it, some of them are upside down and there are duplicates and imposters and comics I didn't even make in there. I can never find the one I'm looking for, in my head or the archive. I use Google to find MY OWN FUCKING COMICS.

Round One
International Waters
Arctic Ocean_

PAINT THE LINE, PART TWO

June 27, 2008 These were so much fun to make, as evidenced by the two people playing Table Tennis on top of a Soviet submarine with a live fish going nuts on there. I don't know if I ever went into it, either on the site or in a book, but this series isn't called *Paint the Line II* for no reason. The first "movie" is alluded to in the crawl, but it's essentially a goofy kind of *Red Dawn* meets Ping Pong. Red Pong? I guess that would be the elevator pitch. I'd love to get that one up on the site someday, or in a book, or do anything at all with *Paint the Line*. I know what happens in the third movie as well, but I want to save that in case we get a chance to do it someday.

PAINT THE LINE, PART THREE

June 30, 2008 Shit's dangerous, kid. But the ocean, is like, that thing's house. If somebody rolled into *your* living room with some kinda Goddamn warship and then had some motherfuckers playing games up on your porch, and your mouth was sufficiently large, or if you were like an Orca or what-ever, maybe this kind of shit would go down. Now, they're supposed to be mad gentle beasts. I read about that somewhere. But they gotta have limits. You know? There's gotta be a breaking point somewhere in there.

PAINT THE LINE, PART FOUR

July 2, 2008 "Oksana Svedlovigoba" is based on a real person—Biljana "Biba" Golić. We met her, actually—it was legitimately terrifying. Terrifying because she was so good at Ping Pong, I mean— she was super nice, even when she was pulping us at the table. We occasionally play tournaments against developers, and Hidden Path (who apparently knew her already) brought her by as a ringer. Robert is very good at this game, as he is at all games, and every activity he chooses to be good at. It didn't matter. He looked like he'd never played before, like he didn't know what the paddle was for, or why someone had attached a net to a perfectly good table.

PAINT THE LINE, PART FIVE

July 4, 2008 It's not a rule or anything, not an explicit one, but romance isn't something we cover in *Penny Arcade* with any regularity. It just doesn't come up a lot, largely because the two people you're most likely to see "on screen" barely like each other and it's strongly implied that they hate each other. Because it's so rare to see any kind of physical contact between characters that doesn't result in decapitation, it's almost more shocking to represent affection in the comic. At the time of this writing there's only really four kisses I can think of in the whole of our history, and fully half of them are between men.

*The standard length of a regulation Ping-Pong table.

PAINT THE LINE, PART SIX

July 7, 2008 Oh, ho! "War wounds," indeed. It's too bad Tycho was completely obliterated in re-entry, so we'll never have an opportunity to explore this kind of deep trauma. It's a shame that no sample survived re-entry so that no clone could be created by the brightest Soviet minds, no new Tycho grown in a laboratory to be brainwashed and trained to regard his country of origin as an amoral, Darwinian hellhole where only the least virtuous succeed. It is a shame, too, that there's no scenario by which Gabriel and Tycho could be made to do battle for "all the marbles" atop a sequence of ruined, global landmarks.

PAINT THE LINE, PART SEVEN

July 9, 2008 Ooh; the coveted double strip. Rare. Not Kiss rare, but rare nonetheless. We think of ourselves as commentators first, as opposed to storytellers, so whenever the second one begins to supersede the former we start to get antsy. Around the end of a story, the urge to collapse two strips into a single day (provided Gabriel has the "bandwidth" to do so) just gets a little too strong. We like to tell stories, now much more than in the past, and people seem to like when we do it, but when you're in the middle of some two week thingamabob like this the world doesn't stop. There's

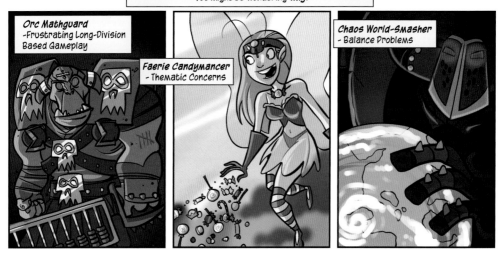

SELECTIVE SERVICE

July 11, 2008 *Song Summoner* was a game that took the tracks on your iPod and turned each of them into a fierce warrior. Or, attempted to. Like personal favorites *Audiosurf*, *Vib Ribbon*, or the by now positively ancient *Monster Rancher*, it gave you a mechanism to derive even more enjoyment from your shit, which is an inherently noble goal. *Monster Rancher* especially, out of that group— I don't know if anybody still thinks about that game aside from me. It occupies a special place in my memory; I racked up something like eighty dollars in late fees on that game.

THE WHEAT/CHAFF RATIO

July 14, 2008 To make a launch in 2008 anything close to conceivable, there were big cuts made to *Warhammer: Age Of Reckoning* around this time. Or maybe the cuts were made long before, but we were just hearing about it then. I'm a pretty big fan of Games Workshop, which is something that's come through in a couple strips—most overtly in the comic titled "I Hope You Like Text"—and it was fun to play around with their stuff here. I think about that Mathguard a lot, even today. Gabriel killed the art on it, just brutal stuff, and the Abacus Sword that dude has is something I want to own.

IT'S JUST LIKE BEING THERE

July 16, 2008 What a bizarre generation this has been. The Wii was the jewel of the industry until something... shifted, and the system fell through a crack in the earth. Microsoft has apparently found some kind of success by becoming the box du jour for hardcore shooters, while positioning the hardware wherever they can as something for every sentient creature. The takeaway of the last eight years over at Sony, the standout piece of information, is a kind of unshakable pride. It's at odds with their performance, but the puffing and strutting has been constant. It seemed they'd created a kind of Dynasty with the first two Playstations; that's what most people believed. They believed it, too.

THE MAN-MAKER

July 18, 2008 The original video is gone now, I think he might have closed his account, which I sort of understand. Most people, wisely, have no interest in being a Public Person. You can still find this thing, though: run a search for "halo kid cardboard" and you'll pull up one of the existing mirrors. I just watched it again, and it's still incredible! He built himself an entire MJOLNIR suit. The way this young man mimics the animations in the game—up to and including the infamous Teabag—is frame for frame. It's uncanny to see them leap into terrifying reality. Fuck Star Wars kid, Star Wars kid can go to hell.

VACILLATION STREET

July 21, 2008 I knew that achievements—often styled "cheevos," cheeves," or on rare occasions "Rick Cheeves"—were effective at manipulating people, but I didn't understand exactly how good they were at it, or the service they perform for publishers and platform holders. These are people who essentially worship data, clean data, unsullied by the bursts of static that almost uniformly accompany any kind of self-reporting. They now know exactly how many people are finishing their games, how far they actually got, how long it took to get there, how many people chose male or female avatars, all of it. I wonder how it's changing the games they make.

SAN DIEGO SKETCHBOOK: ON VIBROBLADES

July 23, 2008 Our scanner broke one year, and with the improvements in cellphone cameras we started just making comics any old place we could find, on any surface that was available. I think the kind of thing you see above is novel, an intrusion of comics into the Prime Material plane—we typically just leave the art on whatever public surface we snapped the shot on, as though art were a naturally occurring substance. It's entirely possible that people consider this sort of thing as an interruption of service, and there's a case to be made for it; these days, we try to do a couple strips ahead of time.

SAN DIEGO SKETCHBOOK: INTIMACY

July 25, 2008 The oddities of our mysterious, borderline romantic union have already filled many pages, in many books, and also our entire comic is a kind of will they/won't they exercise when viewed at a certain angle. There is, in fact, a robust community of enthusiasts who investigate precisely this theme in what I would describe as an exhaustive way. But in real life, we prefer to think of each other as Ken Dolls, absolutely smooth on the front, with no discernible biology and absolutely no use for a bathroom. The truly bizarre construction of our shared hotel room made this impossible; I could literally smell his urethra.

SAN DIEGO SKETCHBOOK: FELICITOUS

July 28, 2008 I mean, it's not entirely a joke; like any other ugly, fat, bald person, I have reason to believe people will be naturally and understandably repulsed if I can't keep a steady stream of anecdotes and canny observations going. This only gets worse if you are meeting a rad person, which at San Diego Comic-Con is not an If proposition, but a When, and Felicia Day is absolutely at that tier. She came to PAX the very next year, and having seen this strip she brought with her a brush specifically for grooming purposes. This was a surprise, seeing as that part of the strip *was* a joke. But you don't turn something like that down.

LONG, LONG AGO

July 30, 2008 This was when *Soul Calibur* was going in for another round of exclusive characters, this time drawn from *Star Wars* for some reason (?!?) which elevated platform preference to the kind of angst and drama we associate with German opera. We've seen pro-level play in this game, and that is not us, but independent of their strange origin we found the characters pretty interesting. Yoda is sorta doing his Episode II flip out and get wild with Dooku type shit, and Vader had a clear role and a fun moveset.

THE TENDER HUMAN TRACHEA

August 1, 2008 Two *Soul Calibur* strips in a row means that it must have taken root, though Gabriel and I didn't last as long as some in the office did. Robert and Kiko played the game for years, as in, more than one year, which (given how we hop feverishly from title to title) is a pretty impressive feat. They just carved a half-hour out of every day, 4:30 sharp, and their approaches changed radically over this period. The "champion" changed rarely, but the shifts were momentous. Robert was able to succeed for a while by adding a random—literally, random—attack every now and then. It was fascinating to watch them; it was like a private zoo.

THE ONGOING SAGA

August 4, 2008 This is a very strange job. Not writing comics, and then writing the book *about* the comics you wrote before, although that's weird too but you get used it. No, I mean being the steward of a perpetually molting psyche. Gabriel and I have different approaches in this regard, as is suggested by the strip, but my allegiance to "truth" doesn't involve positing or even gesturing at the possibility of slavering wolfoids. The reality is that my son is scared shitless on the regular by the news and food poisoning and Alzheimer's and the omnipresent possibility of an aneurism. A bipedal wolf I could simply wave away would be a tremendous relief.

ANGUISH.JPG

August 6, 2008 People were putting together their own takes on *Diablo III* screenshots at this time, ones which contrasted grimy sex dungeons with the new look, which they called "wow gayness." The game came out only recently, so looking at this ancient row over their aesthetic here in my scrying pool is hilarious. At the end of the day, the look of the game wasn't the problem at all. It wouldn't really matter how it looked. The game was simply too smooth, too engineered. There was never anything to get stuck on. It was beautiful, absolutely. And I looked at it. But then I wanted to play a videogame.

FOR YOUR CONSIDERATION

August 8, 2008 This is still true. STILL TRUE. People are, rightly, concerned with the efficiency of their leisure dollar. But this concern seems to become amplified the less something costs; the vigilance becomes hypervigilance. The only time this doesn't apply is when something costs less because it's on sale. Then it's time to buy! When we had a Steam Sale of *On The Rain-Slick Precipice Of Darkness 3* a couple months after launch, daily purchases increased something like five thousand percent. Five thousand! And that's going from five dollars, to three! It's easy to get a big multiple of a small number, but still. Crazypants.

GEARS OF CONFLICT RESOLUTION

August 11, 2008 You could already turn the blood into... not blood, but altering the language tracks as well I thought was interesting. I mused in the strip that a version of *Gears of War* without blood and without cussin' probably wasn't M rated anymore. I don't know what kind of a rating you get for pushing a flamethrower into someone's chest and then roasting them internally, though; maybe that's still "Mature." In any case, I wondered if there's ever going to be a time where there is value in releasing two versions of a game at different ratings. It depends on who is actually purchasing games—parents, or their savage teens.

EFFICIENCY

August 13, 2008 There are simply some fundamental disconnects between the kinds of quests that make up a normal MMO and the fundamental assumptions of *Star Trek* as a universe. There's just a lot of shit those people don't have to put up with, because one of the machines on their ship has completely obviated some species of human misery. I played in the Beta, when things were kinda goofy, but never ended up playing the full version. It's free to play now, so I guess there's nothing really stopping me from getting in there other than a *full-year backlog of world-class electronic entertainment.*

"I'M counting that as a stroke."

BOGEY GOLF, PART ONE OF THIRTY

August 15, 2008 The "Part One Of Thirty" up there is a joke. It's a joke! You didn't just buy a book full of Golf comics. Gabriel loves this stuff, for really, and he's sort of dedicated 2012 to rededicating himself to the sport. Making Golf Comics professionally is something he would do in a heartbeat. There would be no decision, there. I would just come in to work one day, and he would be gone.

"There's no dog fucking in golf!"

BOGEY GOLF, PART TWO OF THIRTY

August 18, 2008 Now, it may be that our comic sensibilities are out of step with the readership of *Golf Digest*. Then again, it's possible those leathery fucking coots might "take a shine" to our special brand of "zip-zoom." These comics, as many of them as we planned to do, surrounded the launch of the next Tiger Woods game. It was a good one! It allowed us to play online sometimes, which we appreciated.

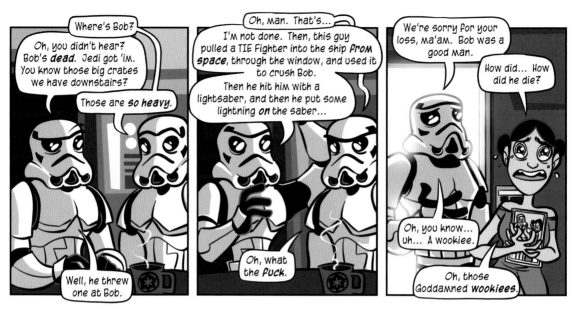

A LIFE OF SERVICE

August 20, 2008 You know what's weird? I enjoyed this strip, enjoyed writing it and reading it, enjoyed the art, but it wasn't until just now that I realized what a clever thing he'd done with the masks. The top of the visor as some kind of mutable eyebrow?! I'm in love. We occasionally come to (figurative) blows over what is worthy content for a panel, and I generally suggest that they should be filled with increasingly complex ironic diagrams. He usually wants some kind of "art." But these Stormtroopers could have been hum and/or drum, and he found a way to amuse himself. We could take these two pretty far, if we wanted; office comedies are in.

YE OF LITTLE FAITH

August 22, 2008 I felt compelled to like *Mirror's Edge*, because it had rad art and the demo fucking rocked balls, but I found the game itself super frustrating. Recall that Electronic Arts was considered the devil back then, as opposed to Activision; and seeing them plow money into new brands like *Dead Space* and *Mirror's Edge* was good for the heart. I vastly preferred their time trials over the campaign, though—little bits of platforming I could perfect. It's a game about momentum, and I could never maintain it in the missions. Apropos of the strip, though, I'm not entirely sure "parkour" is a reliable shipping method.

Alright, so, you know how I went over to yell at our new neighbor for cutting the cable? And destroying our Internet? And sending us back to the Stone Age?

That didn't happen.

What? You said you were going to "regulate"!

I was fucking intimidated! His whole house was full of stuffed animals! I don't mean, like, fucking Build-A-Bear. I mean, like fucking *real* animals. It was like the Galactic Senate, but... all *deer heads*.

So, what did happen?

I agreed that we would go hunting this weekend.

Hunting for what? *Bargains?*

Animals, I guess? Or people? I don't know! It wasn't really clear.

THE WOODS, PART ONE

August 25, 2008 We are called upon to be "men" sometimes, to negotiate with strange neighbors or to pop elbows back in or to otherwise engage in Rambovian behavior. We are not well suited to it. The first part of this series is quite true, that there was some kind of serious interpersonal, intercabular dispute, and despite his polished and vigorous words to the contrary no "regulation" was forthcoming. Everything that happens after that we made up, which is better than how it actually went down.

THE WOODS, PART TWO

August 27, 2008 It may surprise you to learn, or maybe it won't surprise you, this is something I can't know, but I had vests of various kinds and hunting licenses and I can shoot guns reasonably well. I like to eat animals; that's a thing I'm always doing, or about to do. They have tons of meat in there, which must be super inconvenient. If there was another way to get the meat out, I think we would probably do that instead. If you want to think very, very hard about this problem, read *The Sparrow* by Mary Doria Russel.

THE WOODS, PART THREE

August 29, 2008 Jesus Christ, these things get weird when its time to wind them down.

THE JOCONJUGAL VISIT

September 2, 2008 Jonathan Coulton is the very best, and his beautiful modifications to the itinerant folkster mold are well known by now. I saw him at a fundraiser for 826—check them out, it's super cool—and I said, immediately, that we needed to get that fucker to PAX. We wondered to what extent his unique approach had modified the understood "groupie" model: what would *his* clandestine en-counter schedule look like? It'd be broad, we determined. And he'd never let a thing like "not being a person" or "being an actual robot" get in the way.

THE GABRIEL EFFECT

September 3, 2008 Let me tell you a story about the kind of shit these fields of his are still able to pull off. We ordered a computer from Online Computer Manufacturer Dot Com, we've ordered lots of stuff from them, including my own computer, and it's a fucking monster. We had to send his computer back four separate times to get it replaced. Something new every time. Nothing out of the blue, I mean that something was fucked every time we pulled it out of the box. Eventually he flipped out, we sent the machine back and told them to keep it. He decided to order a machine from Universally Recognized Computer Brand. THIS COMPUTER WAS FUCKED ALSO!

MAZELTOV, HUMAN WIZARD

September 5, 2008 He's all dungeon lord supreme now, *now*, but back then—in the period between the *WoW TCG* and starting up his own game just a couple months later—he was still playing "iron-ically." He jumped into my group on a lark, as a kind of performance art or something, and I think that it ended up planting a seed or two. Specifically, in the game he was in, he went off the rails: far, far outside the bounds of the night's adventure plan. The Dungeon Master just ran with it, and it was as much or *more* fun than the actual menu. When you're used to regular games and then you see something like that, there's a *click* upstairs.

A CARNIVAL OF DELIGHTS

September 8, 2008 This was the fucking best, no joke, and I wish it would come back. I bear the young people at Gamestop no ill will, but it's the official policy of the company to operate itself in the most profoundly annoying way possible. I buy games in department stores now as a rule not because I *like* doing it but because they don't fuck with me. They don't prevail upon my shit re: games that come out months later or any other crap. That's what it was like at 7-Eleven, except I could also get gas and beer, and the people at the register did not give a SHIT about street dates. Hmm; that last part may be connected in some way with its mysterious disappearance.

INFINITE TIGER

September 10, 2008 Alright, so, now that we were actually able to *play* Tiger Woods online, we rarely had the opportunity to play it *against* anyone who wasn't Tiger Woods. For years, now, the game has had this crazy sophisticated suite of tools to create custom golfers you can then perfect, RPG style, into a terrifying robogolfer. You can take pictures of yourself and make a little sporting doppelganger person and dress them in pretty clothes. It sort of seems like the whole point of the game. But then you'd go into multiplayer, and for some inexplicable reason they would allow people to choose this comically potent golf sorcerer in competitive matches.

THE DIPLOMATIC ROUTE

September 12, 2008 A scenario that happens from time to time runs something like this: an event occurs that we think will make for a good comic, but it will involve the revelation of information that could get one or both of us into trouble. This was that, absolutely. I don't even remember what it was, now, what kind of bow it was, but at that moment in time it was *the* bow. It was the bow you knew about even if you didn't use bows, had no predilection toward bows; even if you rolled a Pally you knew about this motherfucker. You'd see it twinkling out on the bridge in Ironforge, and you'd covet it, even though the Bible explicitly calls that a no-no.

CONSENSUS

September 15, 2008 They're no doubt lost to time, now, but the truly nasty Microsoft Vista rolled out alongside these stunted, awful *Seinfeld* things. We're in love with *Seinfeld*, *Seinfeld* isn't the problem; these were just... pointless. They have an uphill battle selling a new version of their operating system to people whose computers currently work. I said at the time that this was part of why I was impressed at what they'd managed with the Xbox 360, suggesting that "trying to associate Microsoft with 'fun' was like trying to associate Satan with aromatherapy." Advertising doesn't drive me nuts as a rule, but bad advertising makes me homicidal.

WHY, INDEED

September 17, 2008 This strip was produced to commemorate a trip to the Puyallup Fair, which, if you are not from around here, is a kind of Fair that we have. We've got baked beans and elephant ears in the first panel, just in case these are not native to your region. The beans are like the beans you know already, but amplified in a mysterious device. At PAX East, they have something called Fried Dough which is like an Elephant Ear—it's relief map of fried bread dripping with fat, cinnamon, and sugar. This was also an opportunity to write dialect, and I have a solid handle on this particular fork of the language, which I call "jailmouth."

THINKING SMALL

September 19, 2008 LucasArts had a game called *Fracture*, and just in case you had sort of forgotten it too, it is a game where you can raise and lower terrain. This is the only thing I remember about it, which makes me feel bad. I mean, I guess they could have done something different on their end to help me remember this game's particular struggle, but they had a lot going on making the rest of the game so I shouldn't put it all on them. Having done it a couple times now, at the most minute scale, even in the prosecution of my satirical duty I have tremendous sympathy for the people who make these impossible things.

Gabriel's Birthday: Around The World

Flying Gabriel Rejoice Festival

Goerbemisdag

Los Dias del Gabriel

THE CHRISTMAS IN SEPTEMBER

September 22, 2008 This is one of my favorite *Penny Arcade* strips of all time, I mean, easily Top 5. It's only a question of where in that five it sits. The Christmas in September—September 25th—is Gabriel's actual birthday, and he makes such a ridiculously big production of it in real life that we've worked this propensity into the strip. But I'm in love with the faux-Norwegian "Goerbemisdag," and the puppet in the first panel is never far from my thoughts. Each panel is another reality, full of its own weird ideas, and I want to go into them and see what else is in there! I really want to know what comes out of the piñata.

THE ORIGIN OF THE CD-KEYS, PART ONE

September 24, 2008 We try to work every employee to death at PAX, and those who survive we usually take somewhere. While we were sequestered in that year's Recreation Bunker, we had a number of people weigh in on the issue of "software piracy" which you may be surprised to note has not been completely eradicated in the five years hence! It is pesky. But we had Brian Crecente in there, some Chris Remo, and a little Daniel James from Three Rings. None of them could fix it either, presumably because they were not smart or fast enough. Maybe if I'd had other guest writers, we'd have put this thing to bed.

THE ORIGIN OF THE CD-KEYS, PART TWO

September 26, 2008 Having been a player of games during this period, where dongles existed, but also ridiculously easy piracy, there is a romantic cast to the period. I'd get piles of games for nothing from family members, frontloaded with incredible feats of coding prowess from a global hacker community. I'd get BBS numbers passed to me at school, connecting to boards whose boughs drooped with illicit fruit. Does that describe a common "life cycle" for a gaming enthusiast? A larval phase of ravenous, practically speaking *illegal* hunger, passing into adulthood as a lifelong, paying customer? I honestly don't know.

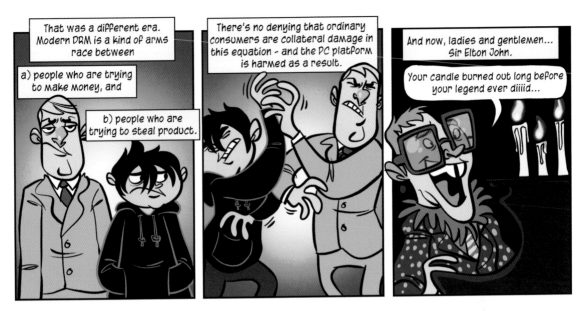

THE ORIGIN OF THE CD-KEYS, PART THREE

September 29, 2008 That's the way I generally put it, when asked: that draconian digital rights management schemes are collaborations between pirates and publishers. I would never say that these methods are effective, indeed, quite the opposite. Only people who purchase software legitimately suffer under this kind of regime. And the publishers which do best under it aren't those who leverage the most brutal "protection," but those who sell "services" instead of "products." Those who sell living software, those who build rapport with the customer. There are lots of ways to do that, but the pro-tip is that it never begins by assuming bad faith.

"The Mega Man 9 Effect"

A TRICK OF RETROSPECTIVE

October 1, 2008 You can order a print of any strip on the site, we're set up to do that. You can, of course, print them at home also. That is not something that keeps me up at night. But if you want it printed out for framing and also if you want that shit to be mad crisp, it's a service we provide. Anyhow, the strip people ask for the most—far, far and away—is this one. In the version we have for printing, we removed the game reference altogether so it's just the two of them transforming into children which is the point of the comic anyway. We happened to be playing *Mega Man 9* at the time, but the strip is much bigger than one game.

THIS IS WHY THEY HATE US

October 3, 2008 When the product launched each flavor had a genre prefix for some reason, like "Action Pizza" or "Sports PB&J." I don't know what the situation is with that, like, if it's okay to play an action game while eating the one formulated for sports. I don't know if it's dangerous, or what. I don't know what the dealio is. I checked to see if these grubs were still being manufactured, and apparently they are—but they've dropped the genres, so gamers need not worry about inauspicious, potentially lethal combinations. The site suggests that this "performance snack" (?) is packed with "neurotransmitters," so... That's good, I guess.

BEHOLD!

October 6, 2008 He doesn't get them from typing things in at random, but he does have an incredible capacity for securing keys. Over the course of our unlikely career he's forged alliances with fellow misanthropes the world over, and when the time comes to reel one in it never takes too long. Gabriel and his boy—also named Gabriel, after... himself, sort of but not really—played the everloving shit out of *Little Big Planet*. No doubt it was that first taste of a mutable environment that primed the young man for *Minecraft*, which has become a favorite escape. The shit this kid does with Redstone Dust is nutballs.

MAGNUM OPUS

October 8, 2008 We expected there to be *mad* peepees from hell to breakfast on *Little Big Planet*, peepees a go-go, but that's not what we saw. Maybe it's overgrowed now with prongs of every conceivable manufacture, but when we were in there—in the Beta of all things, which should have been a haunted realm—it was very humane. Maybe Media Molecule was very good at moderating it, or maybe their weird toy simply attracted a community that was a cut above. The experience was the same, in any case: browsing and playing level after level made you feel like you'd been inducted into a happy, life affirming digital cult.

THE GREAT DIVIDE

October 10, 2008 I suppose it's like the hunger political commentators have for The Independent Voter, that magical individual everyone can project their fondest wishes onto. That Non-Gamer, they're sure will be the future of games. The reality is that "non gamers" are a dwindling pool. Games are how *every* person puts off work, they're how all kinds of people connect and stay in touch. Their "gaming system" also takes calls. If traditional gamers don't like your game, that's a different problem. Consider courting them, though; I have it on good authority that they purchase and play games on occasion.

THE DELUGE

October 13, 2008 *Dead Space* was part of the same "make new shit" initiative that brought us *Mirror's Edge*, and maybe even *Dante's Inferno*. It wasn't a barn burner right out the gate but it seems to have escaped their fate, with one (arguably improved) sequel and another one on the way—it needed time, and iteration, and to their credit they spent the money. They "went hard" on *Dead Space* from the get-go, with reams of tie-in stuff that was a cut above the typical mercenary fare. People say that there's a lot of veiled references to Scientology in it, but, um... I'm not sure these references of theirs are all that veiled.

THE BREAKING POINT

October 15, 2008 Being a parent who is also a huge dork has a unique texture. There are a lot of "learnings." For example: when our own fathers were trying to make us do things that we did not like, or were dumb, they wanted us to understand their deal. They were "speaking" through these activities! It's something you'll catch yourself doing if you ever end up in this job, trying to stuff your larvae into a mold which is curiously shaped like yourself. I have faith that my interests *are* rad, and that my progeny will arrive at them in due course independent of any protracted sales effort.

BRUTAL DIPLOMACY

October 17, 2008 He doesn't know Karate, that's true. He knows T'ai chi ch'uan, or he did—he used to be completely over the moon for it, in another phase of the site where the now illusory "free time" was in greater supply. He had those awesome pants and the awesome shirt with the long buttons that you see Jet Li wearing in those vaguely historical Kung-Fu costume dramas. He can "Part The Wild Horse's Mane" if I remember correctly. He can also hit you with something called a Bloodfist. He hasn't really been forthcoming with any of the specifics, but I want to put this out there: it seems bad.

A VALID LINE OF INQUIRY

October 20, 2008 Because the strip and Really Real Life intersect in strange and occasionally surprising ways, I feel compelled to announce that—while I like animals—I don't *like* like them. But it keeps coming up in the strip, so it would be totally legitimate for you to wonder why that might be. While there are comics which consist of direct transcriptions, in general "Tycho" and "Gabe" are exaggerations of ourselves on every axis—both positive and negative. Gabriel finds my Bookmarks to be a terrifying realm, one I used to expose him to with regularity, until it was easier never to look at my screen. These strips are about that.

A BROKEN CLOCK

October 22, 2008 It didn't end up on the evening news, probably because it was a little inside baseball. I'd forgotten completely about the fact that LPB (which is what "the kids" call *Little Big Planet*) had been recalled. Do you remember why? It was because one of the songs they'd licensed included two verses from the Qur'an. There's a lot I don't know about the world! In the religion I grew up in, this sort of shit happens constantly. You would probably get in trouble if you *didn't* sing the verses! Then again, my religion thought you would go to hell if you listened to heavy metal. Everybody's dealing with their own stuff.

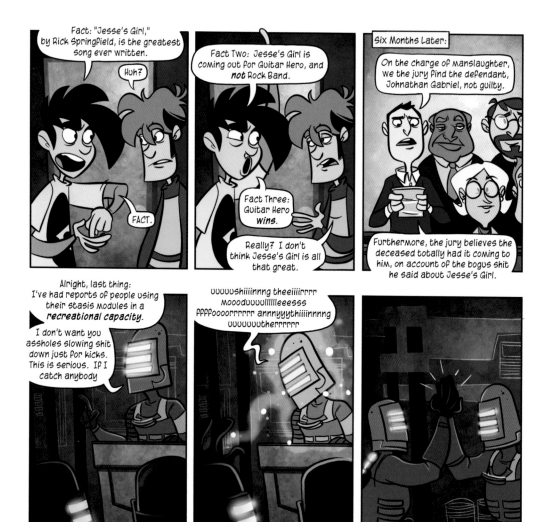

THE VERDICT

October 24, 2008 Fucking with him as regards his music selections is a time honored pastime, both in the strip and in the greater world. But this is something I just let him have.

FUN WITH MODULES

October 27, 2008 One of my favorite things about *Dead Space* is one of my favorite things about any good science fiction: it tries to answer the basic questions in a consistent way. I'm not the sort of person who needs to know precisely how long a Super Star Destroyer is in order to enjoy *Star Wars*, or by what precise biological mechanism the Force operates; you can get into the weeds pretty quickly answering things like that, until you actively dilute wonder and mystery. But the explanations for your weapons and technology all helped ground you in the setting, and in the character. He doesn't want to be there. And neither do you.

THE LOCAL COLOR

October 29, 2008 I've liked basically all the newer *Tomb Raider* reboots—I think Crystal Dynamics is doing the Lord's work. Legend especially offers up a tender bit of retroactive continuity that puts Lara's tireless spelunking efforts in a coherent, dare I say, touching context. She definitely goes nuts on the wildlife, but the stress she's under is incredible, and a lot of those species have never been catalogued so it's not like anyone is going to miss them. My favorite *Tomb Raider* game doesn't even have *Tomb Raider* in the title: it's *Lara Croft and the Guardian of Light*. Nobody seems to know how great this thing is, and it's bizarre.

OPERATION MYRIAD

October 31, 2008 When we started going into a spreadsheet/calendar to plan *in absolute specificity* the minute by minute breakdown of an entire month, we began to realize that we were engaged in the most ridiculous kind of activity possible. It was at that point that—and this is not without precedent—we decided to humiliate ourselves publically for your benefit. They pack product in like this for a reason, I mean, I've talked to people at the helm of this shit and they have shown me their magical graphs. But in the environment we've got right now—where one miss sinks a studio—I wonder how long this game of chicken can continue.

PERHAPS SLIGHTLY EXAGGERATED

November 3, 2008 Alright, so, even if you wanted to play *Mirror's Edge*, and its concerns did not concern *you*, there is a chance that you might still throw up. The urge to hyperlink the words "throw up" is very strong, but I'm not writing this for a computer, and sometimes I have to remind myself. As a first person platformer, a "genre" only a handful of people have ever really attempted, it's got some camera tricks to place you in the frame and make sure that you are nauseated. I got through it alright, but this happens from time to time; my body is different from Gabriel's. Well, some parts are the same. But he can't really see 3D stuff, either; it's been a problem.

PROVE ME WRONG

November 5, 2008 I'm not sure what he's got me drinking in that last panel; the skull seems like a bad indicator. But I keep having an opportunity to talk about this lately, which right now means 2012, but won't be any less valid whenever you read this.

WITH GREAT VENGEANCE

November 7, 2008 I have scrupulously avoided Facebook. I have an account, because they will hunt you down if you don't. But I don't spend a lot of time orbiting it because... I don't know why, honestly. I think that if I didn't have *Penny Arcade*, a place where I reveal myself constantly, something like that would fit into my life somewhere. As it stands, I don't want to be exposed any more than I already am, which to my mind seems Goddamned near absolute. Maybe I need to cook up a fake one, just for the games. They're starting to have things we could realistically call a "game," now, as opposed to spooky experiments on the fringe of human conditioning.

THE REALNESS GRADIENT

November 10, 2008 I am Gearhead Supreme, a real nutjob about this kind of stuff. I've even read "the books!" I usually make it a point *not* to read "the books." They were by Karen Traviss, though, who they eventually brought on to write the third game, so they must have liked what she had to say about their universe. I always felt a little silly about the level of my enthusiasm. Sometimes I think I see things in the setting the developer doesn't, and so when I rail on them for not having especially tidy narrative or cornball dialogue it might not be a good investment of a Friday morning. If they're shooting for B-Movie Action, and they're hitting it squarely, maybe I need to let it go.

FUN WITH NANOSCALE METAMATERIALS

November 12, 2008 I'm sure that I could come up with the why. It wouldn't take me long, because... *Gearhead*, as I suggested previously. Let me crack my knuckles, here. Okay: my first guess would be that it's eminently possible, but not especially practical. My second guess would correlate that the devastation of industry and governance on Sera would almost certainly preclude this kind of resource investment at the infantry level. My third guess is that Epic just wanted an excuse not to render the robot all the Goddamned time. Let's go with "C."

LIMITLESS ADVENTURE

November 14, 2008 To a certain extent it doesn't matter. I mean, right? They have the most money, the most robust technology, and essentially created the apex of the genre in 2004. Azeroth is a place, as much as anything else, and it is a place like any other social nexus where you go to meet and do things with friends. The game isn't *about* sentient walrii any more than it is about yeti pelts or copper or any of that other shit. You get back in when an expansion comes out; you get your tabard out of mothballs. You meet back up. Or you should, anyway. I mean, if you want ever want to see your friends again.

SOLITUDE

November 17, 2008 Yes; like I was saying.

THE JUBILANT CULMINATION

November 19, 2008 I don't know if "Happy Endings" are some kind of urban legend, or if it really a kind of ending you can actually get, or what. This is what we were trying to figure out then, and we still don't know. I don't think it's something he was actively seeking. He started going to a massage place on the regular because he likes that sort of thing, and I think he was worried (in a social anxiety way) that it might come up or some shit. If you don't have social anxiety, you might think that this is completely ridiculous, and it *is*, insofar as it's not likely to happen. But logic is no antidote for anxiety; there is no sufficient dose.

THE SERVICES I PROVIDE

November 21, 2008 This was a truly unique case, where there was enough fiddly bits for both of us to get the game we wanted. Whenever it became The Other Game, we'd just pass the controller. Also, *Valkyria Chronicles* is one of the best games ever made. It's a completely original tactics game with a completely original look, backed by large-bore Drama. It's more than worth the price of hardware, and it made a beautiful transition to portables so you can get it however you want. Since there was never a sequel for home consoles, I can only guess it didn't do especially well. That's a sin, and we all bear the punishment.

THE TRUTH IS THE NEW LIE

November 24, 2008 So, we're all well aware that people who work Public Relations have a complicated, sometimes subtle, sometimes overt relationship with the press. What made this story so amazing was that the subtlety evaporated completely and we saw the whirring mechanism that toiled beneath it. The direct quote from PR firm Barrington Harvey was "...we're trying to get the Metacritic rating to be high, and the brand manager in the US that's handling all of *Tomb Raider* has asked that we just manage the scores before the game is out, really, just to ensure that we don't put people off buying the game, basically." Yes! I'll bet you are!

IN MEMORIAM

November 26, 2008 Our friend Wil Shipley (of OmniWeb slash Delicious Monster slash Delicious Library fame) bought the strip appearance we offer at the Child's Play dinner twice—maybe even twice in a row. We tried to do him up right, and another of my favorite strips is one of the ones we did for him. But he really did ask us to lionize his cat in one of them, and he provided a truly wide assortment of inspirational material toward this end. He seemed pleased, and I like to think that Murray was pleased also.

TWISTED CULTURAL WRECKAGE

November 28, 2008 They really were truly awful commercials, but the game itself was a physical expression of psychotic hatred for the gaming public. I had completely forgotten this existed at all, even though it was only a few short years ago. It was a kind of sheath for your DS that granted players Carpal Tunnel Syndrome in seconds This was during that period where Activision was actively trying to obliterate the *Guitar Hero* brand—"exploit" is their word—by making it so ubiquitous that you could never escape it. And you really, really couldn't. My mom got me some *Guitar Hero* pajama pants for Christmas; they ride up a bit, abrading the taint.

IT'S REALLY MORE OF AN INVESTMENT

December 1, 2008 We see these Busts or whatever at San Diego Comic Con every year, and while we absolutely appreciate the craftsmanship on display—craftsmanship which is, in a word, ridonkadonk— I don't have any idea where you put something like this. If I had some kinda of Goddamn hidden room I could hoard these heads, maybe. These Locust heads from *Gears of War* are another thing entirely, though. Even if you had a place exclusively *for* your secret heads, this is not a head you would ever want to look at! I have seen them, and they are incredibly fucking gross. Which is accurate, but still!

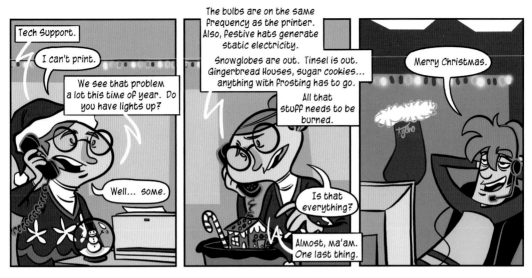

IN DAYS OF YORE

December 3, 2008 The strip title refers to my other life, the one I had when we started *Penny Arcade*— technical support. I worked for a school district, doing rollouts and writing articles for the newsletter and going to sites and banging on broken shit. I don't remember it being a bad job, I remember it being stressful, but everybody I know tells me that the job made me a fucking asshole and I am inclined to believe them. When you're supposed to be "polite" all day, you don't feel like being polite any other time. I had way better health care than I do now, holy shit. A five dollar co-pay is no fucking joke.

WE ARE GATHERED HERE TODAY

December 5, 2008 I loved this game, and I think I was in the minority on this one too. They had to say "Fertile Ground" all the time, because that's where you had to go, and... here, from the post: "It's a term with incredible euphemistic opportunities, but since it's a phrase that denotes game function, the characters have to say it *all the time*. They also pronounce it fur-tile, instead of *ferdl*, which is customary where I live—and I think it's an alien pronunciation for the voice actors too, because every time it comes out of their mouths it is vaguely halting, like they're chewing a mouse."

THE CRISIS

December 8, 2008 This was really a story, I'm not making a joke. This was something people actually talked about for more than a second. You wonder why we can't have nice things? Because we don't deserve nice things, that's why.

SKULDUGGERY

December 10, 2008 He didn't get it for eleven dollars, I'll tell you that much. These things are rare, rare: they're not something you could buy at the time, though I don't know if that's changed now. It's a big, heavy, incredible sculpt of an orc on a riding wolf, or a warg or whatever. It's physically hard to carry. They were only given to employees, and an employee gave it to us for the auction we have at the annual charity dinner. He put it back into circulation with an eBay auction for Child's Play, so it's done a ton of good. And it ain't no worse for wear, neither. It's basically a pile of bronze, you know? It keeps well.

A PENETRATING LOOK

December 12, 2008 Suffice it to say, this is not an experience we returned to for any significant length of time. They would have interesting ideas occasionally, but since they weren't willing to make the experience a core part of their offering for whatever reason your little poppet never gained the currency or stature of a Mii or even an Avatar. One of the weirdest things about it is that it had instanced areas, but not instanced content inside the areas, so games were in limited supply. Digital scarcity! I said in the post that this was "like having the ability to shape being from *non*-being at the subatomic level, and the first thing you decide to make is AIDS."

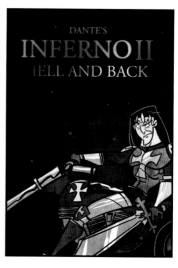

YOU WILL FEEL THE HEAT

December 15, 2008 See, and here it is. It was just weird stuff, and it had boobs in it for some reason, boobs just boobing the whole place up. I would never say that you couldn't make a game about it, or you shouldn't, or that nobody could, but *Dante's Inferno* is *incredibly* high concept. This is a literary assault on... well, just about everything. I really wonder what the process was internally for choosing this "Intellectual Property," because this is a team that we know makes good shit. You know what, this is my mission now. I'm gonna track this down. I won't be able to tell anyone when I find out, but at least I'll know. Ask me if you see me; I'll whisper.

ONCE MORE UNTO THE BREACH

December 17, 2008 He switched back to a PC laptop a year or so ago, an Alienware M14x, which puts an even broader array of social buffers within striking distance. I couldn't figure out what was weirding me out about his array there, but it just hit me a second ago: *physical books*. He's got real books there, as opposed to an endlessly mutable electro-tome that can seize books right out of the air. The *Dungeons & Dragons* supplement didn't phase me, because that's still how that sort of thing is done. For now; for now.

SNOWBALL.EXE

December 19, 2008 No value judgment of course, just sayin', sometimes the weird sort of twilight we exist in is pretty strange. And it won't be getting any less strange as technology improves.

AND SO IT BEGINS, PART ONE

December 22, 2008 I was over at Brenna's parents' house with Elliot, there was no Ronia at this point in time, and Gabriel who is also Mike kept calling me with very specific questions about the game he wanted to run. At first, he didn't even know what books you had to own to *play* the game. Luckily, at that time, they had a three volume set in a nice dust jacket that was an easy recommendation. Specifically, he needed to own the *Players Handbook*, the *Monster Manual*, and the *Dungeon Master's Guide*. How much time have I spent, in how many versions...? It would be terrifying to contemplate.

AND SO IT BEGINS, PART TWO

December 24, 2008 The relationship established in this series is one that we've gotten heaps of strips out of—what you might call the Dungeon Master and Dungeon Apprentice. When we sit down to write comics, it generally just starts out as a kind of unfocused stream that becomes more and more coherent until—optimally—it can bore through tungsten steel. Usually it's best to get any other "business" out of the way first, and when he took up this hobby there was a lot to talk about. It basically took over the writing sessions. That's when it occurred to us that there might be strips *in* tabletop roleplaying games.

AND SO IT BEGINS, PART THREE

December 26, 2008 The idea that he would have ever been nervous about this is so completely insane now. He's far better at it than I ever was, and that isn't merely an attempt to be nice or craft a narrative for events after the fact. He's better at it in every way. What I'm good at—which is another way of saying "what I like to do"—is cook up up the story aspects, embroider the details that give players something to feel and someone to be. I don't think that's Gabriel's favorite part. I think he likes to craft systems and also to make literal crafts. This keeps happening, I guess; we keep having opposite and complementary aptitudes. I don't understand it.

AND SO IT BEGINS, PART FOUR

December 29, 2008 I had this line before we had anything else for this series, it was all the arc we'd take to arrive at it. Especially since everything else had been so earnest and on the nose. Being earnest is fine, and noses are okay, but you can't travel too far from a character in one jump: nobody buys it. Everything else was designed to sell this line. You can read this as Gabe making the kind of adventure that Gabe would make, or that he has been fucking with Tycho the entire time. You can often get a couple reads out of a comic like this, and (as I've said previously) Gabriel and I occasionally disagree on which is the official version.

LIKE A NIGHTMARE, WITH THE DEVIL'S FACE

December 31, 2008 From the post:

"I'm sure it was meant to be grim, but for some reason that story about videogame characters giving men self-esteem issues as well had us in stitches. Part of it may be that we delight in terrible realities, our receptors for joy and despair being reversed—like those creatures who thrive in boiling sea vents or devour toxins, we manifest an alien physiology. We found the idea that it was even possible to like your body *incredibly hilarious*. I've never known a single person whose body was not a source of psychological torment, indeed, it can be seen as the sole conduit of all human suffering. Even in its most pristine condition, the body is a prison. Actually, reading those last two sentences, it occurs to me that *perhaps they are onto something*."

PAINT THE LINE 2

There was a time when we avoided continuity altogether, and said mean things about it, and chastised brigands who used it as a crutch. It turns out, though, that making stories where something happens and then *that* thing makes something *else* happen is kind of fun. People rarely begrudge us these experiments, and occasionally even find them semi-enjoyable. One such person, a man by the name of Steve Bowler, loved *Paint the Line* so much that it inspired him to turn a basic Pong card game he'd prototyped into a full-fledged simulation of global table tennis conflict.

The trouble for him was that he'd never played a real game of Ping Pong before, so, he enlisted our help. Through months of work, he and Kiko designed a card game that has all of the feel of an actual ping pong Cold War Epic without the sore knees, rations, or nuclear fallout drills. All that drama, conveyed through a series of cards?!? It's crazy.

Steve and Kiko banged on the rules until they communicated their vision, and I was only too happy to write the "flavor text" for the cards. That's a type of writing I've always wanted to try my hand at. But the key ingredient in cooking up something like this is heaps and heaps of evocative art. Like, heaps. Way more than Gabe could handle alongside everything else he's got to do. It took a small army of outside artists to make *Red Tide* happen, and we toast them every time we lay down some Stamina and put a card into our Arsenal. We have everything in a much, much higher resolution than is required for the cards, and we thought it would look great in the book. Featuring artwork by Alexandra Douglass, Steve Hamaker, and Alexandria Neonakis.

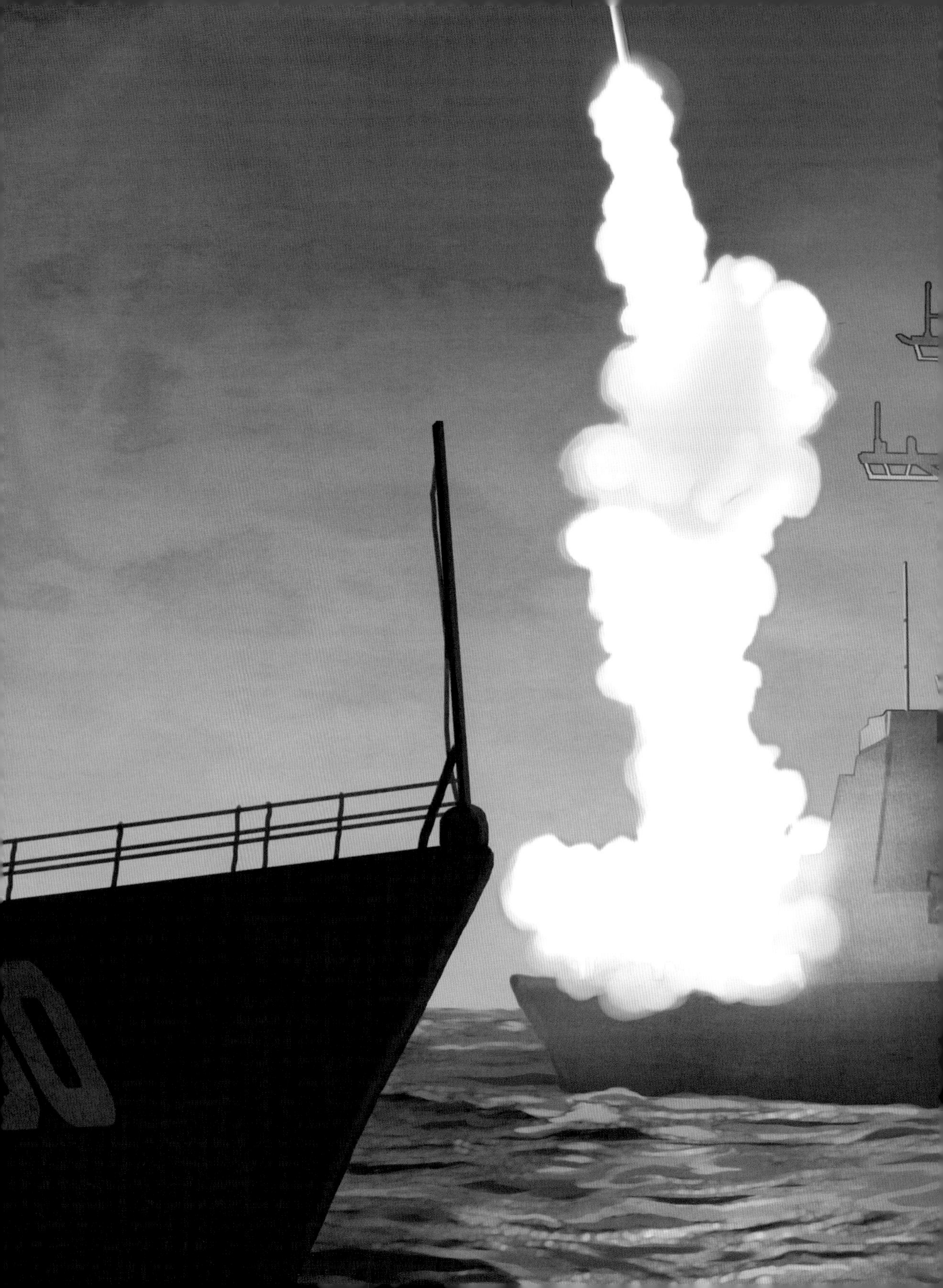

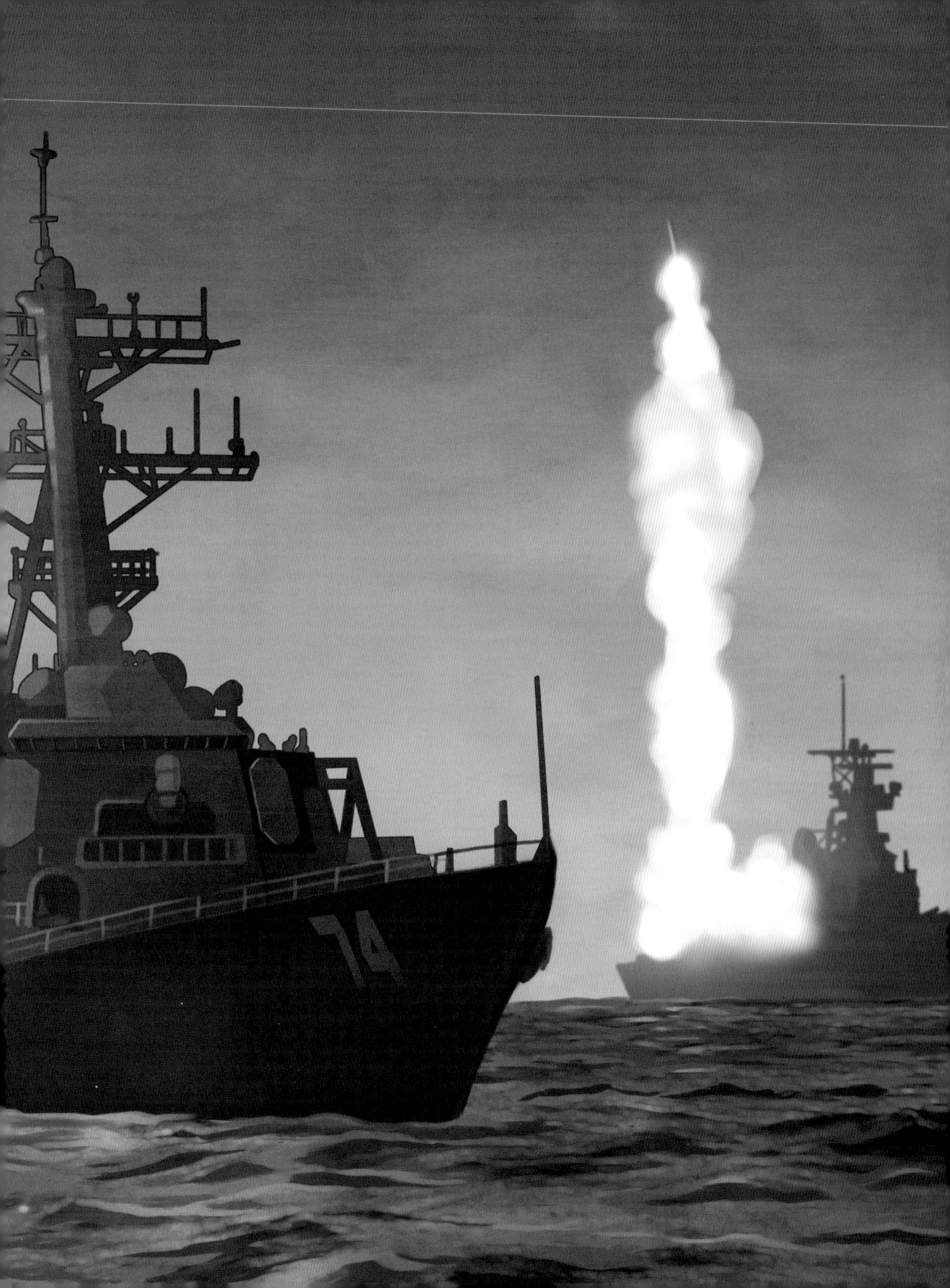
74

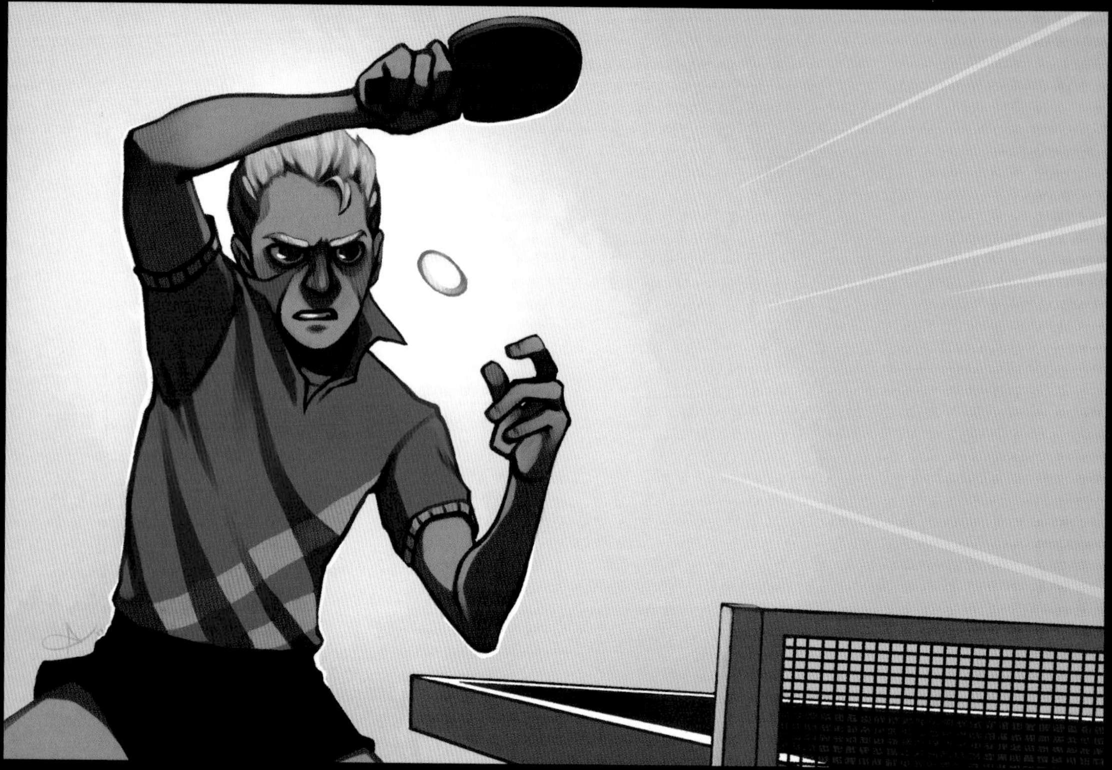

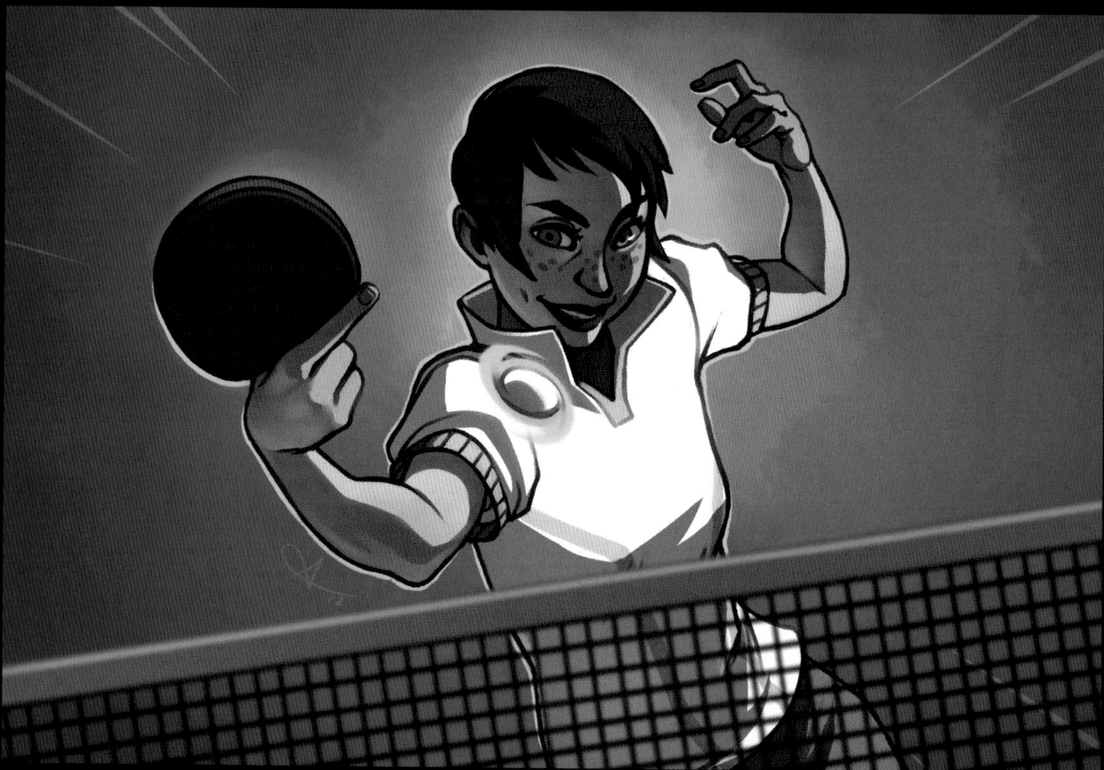

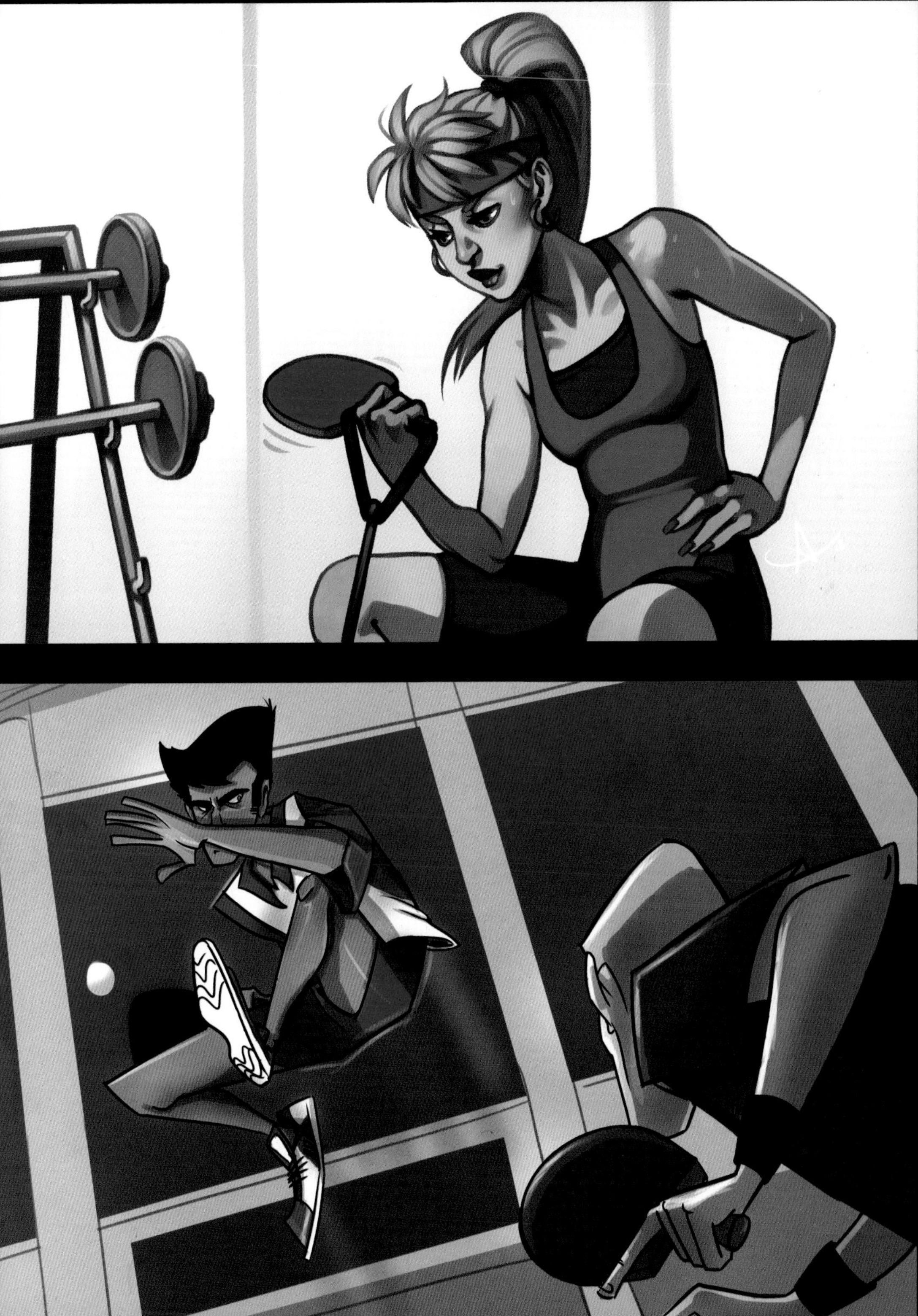

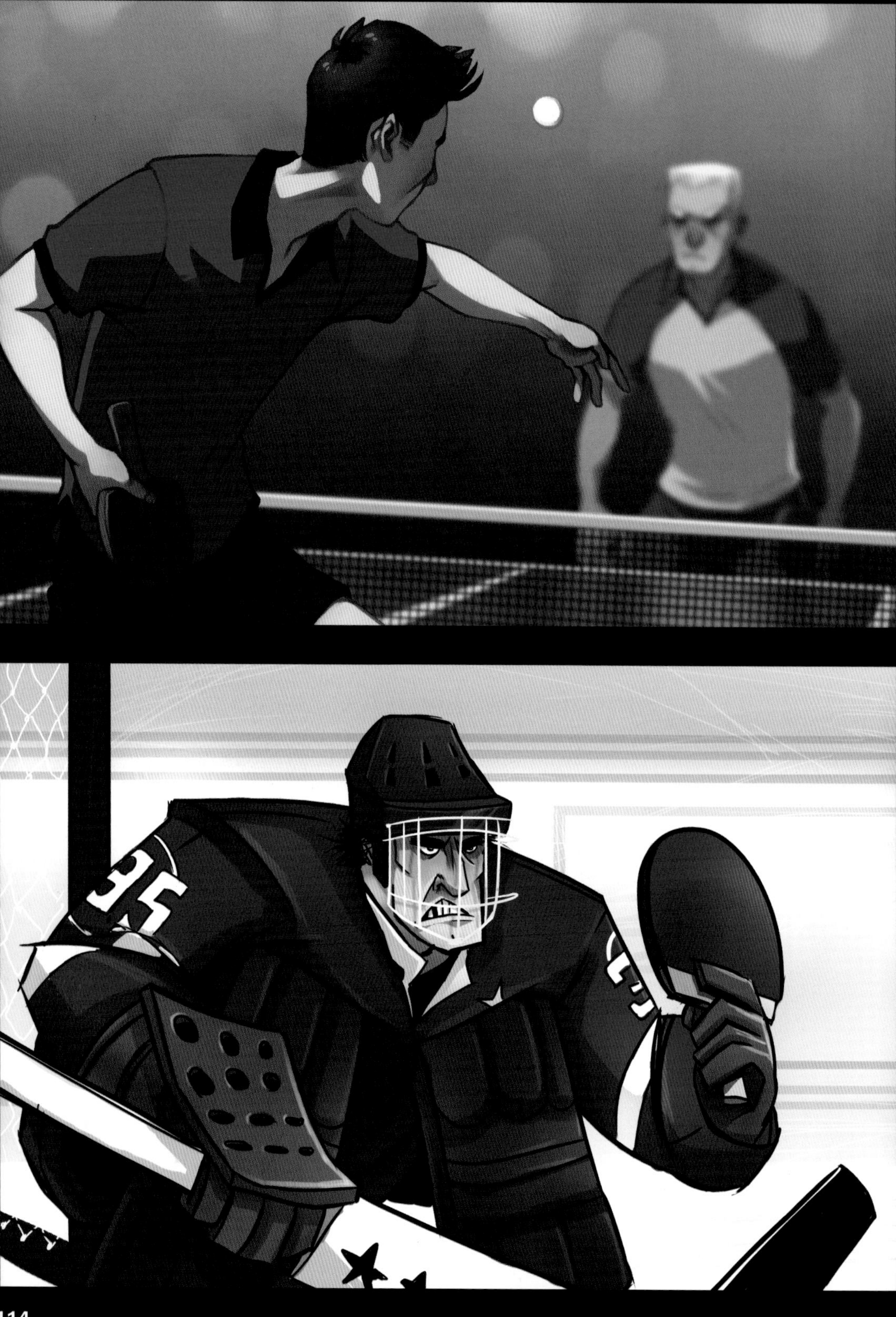
35

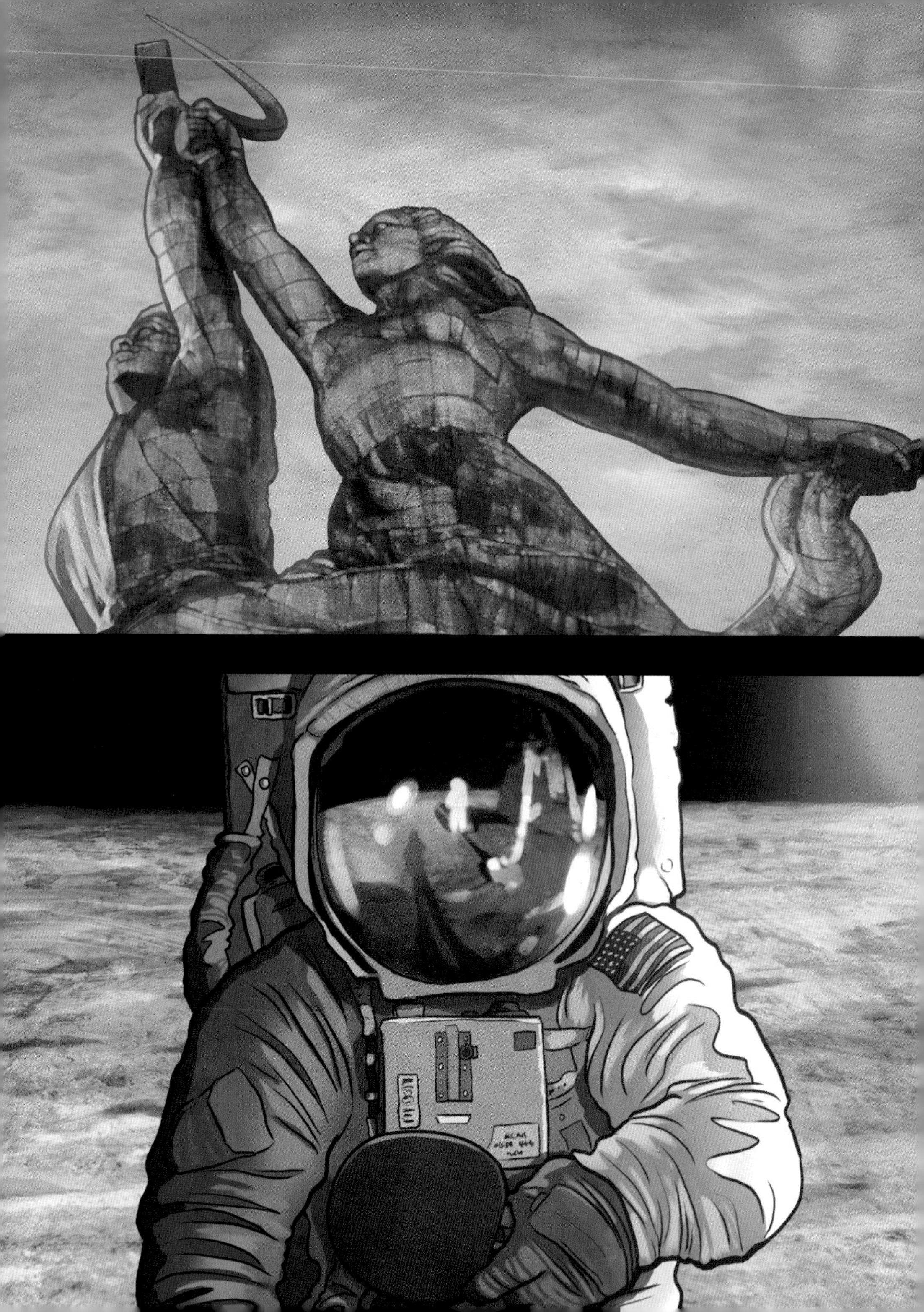

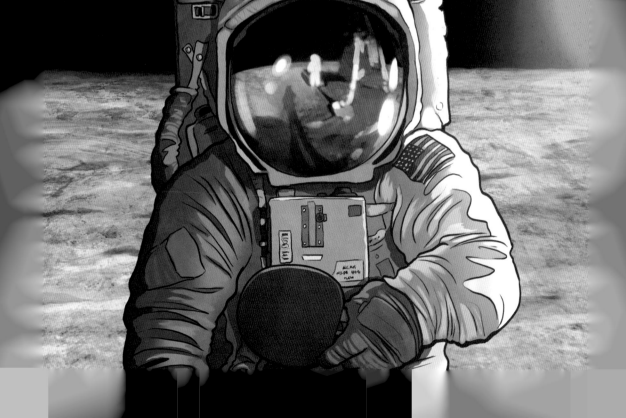

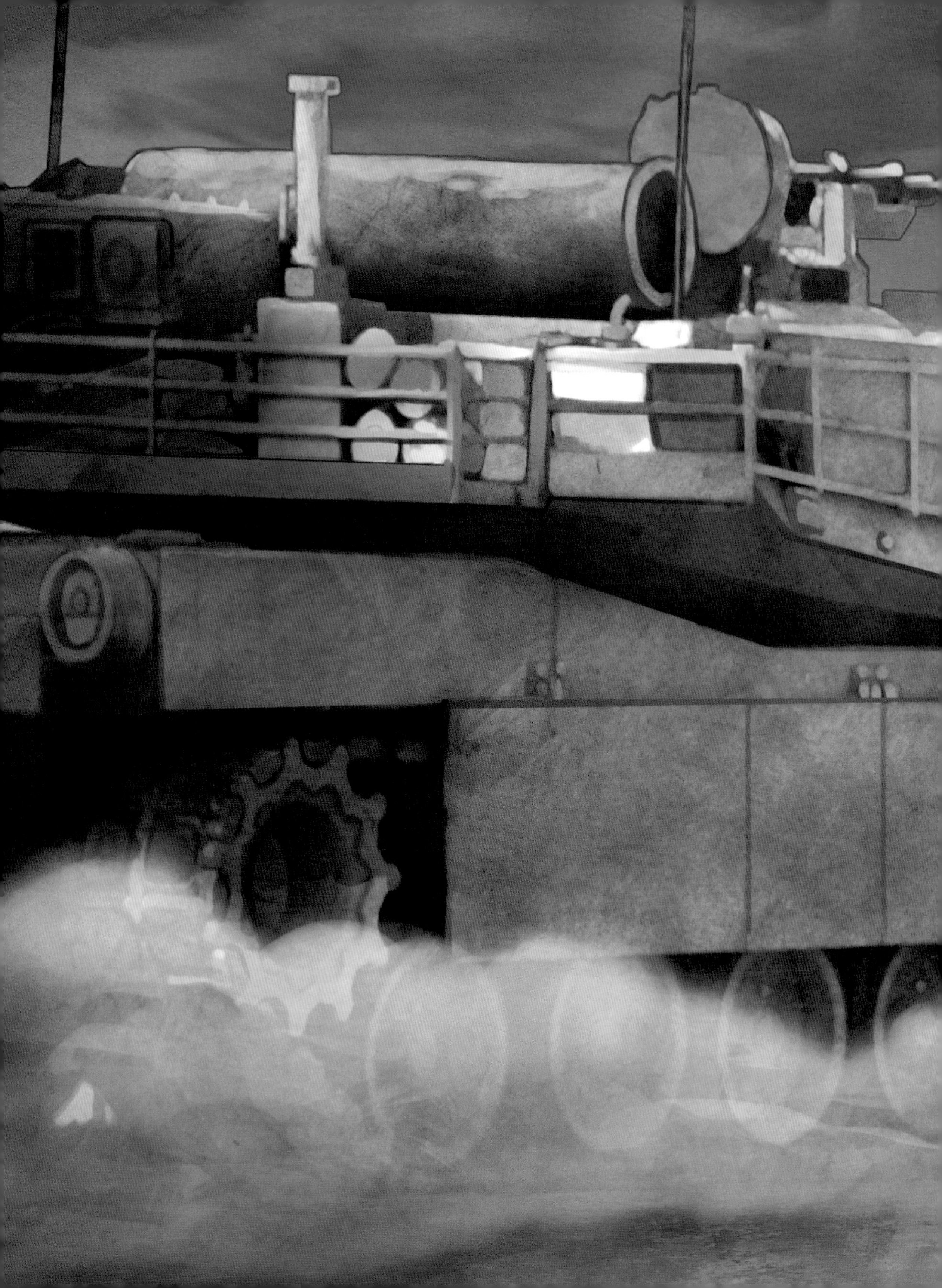

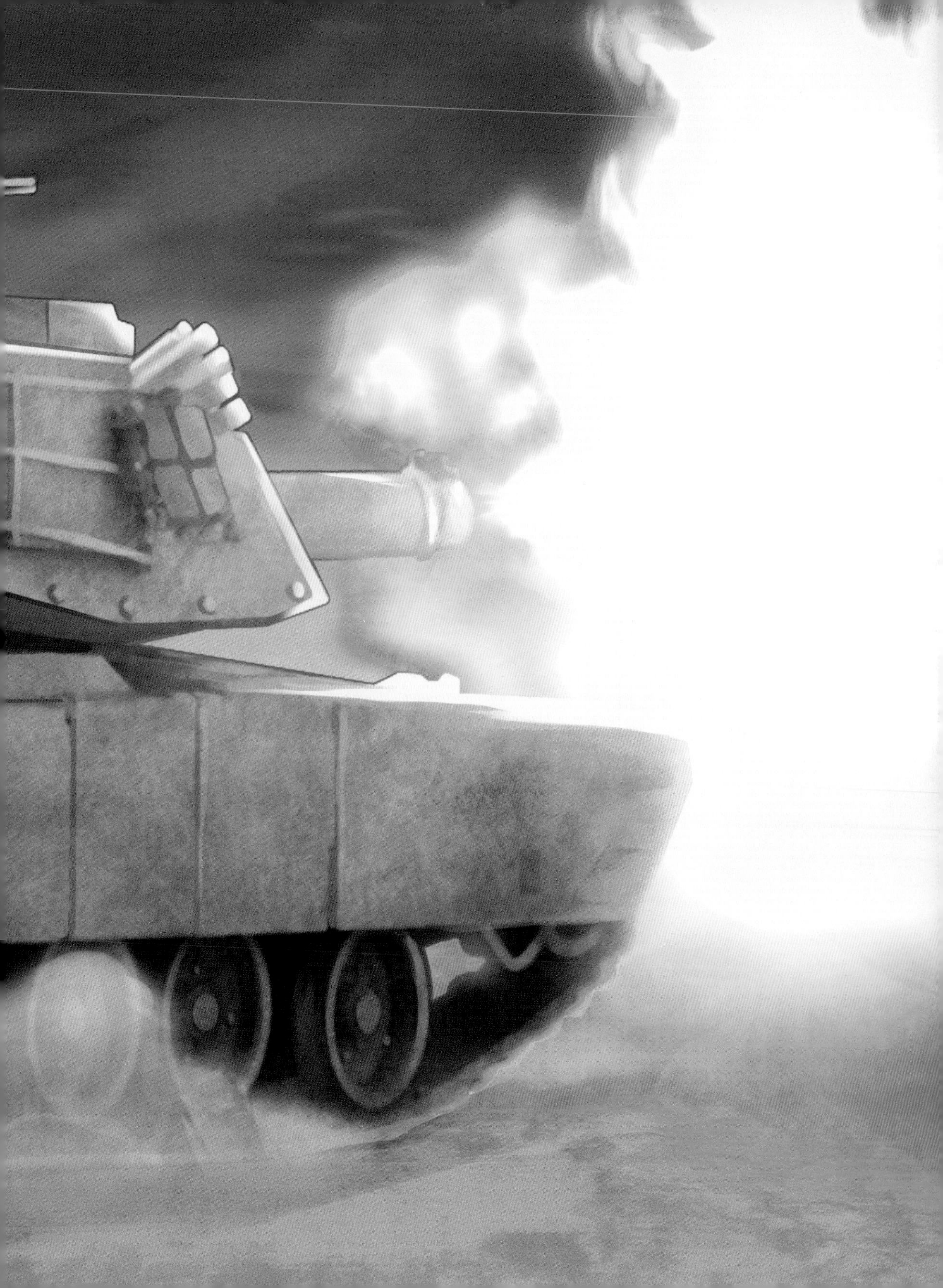

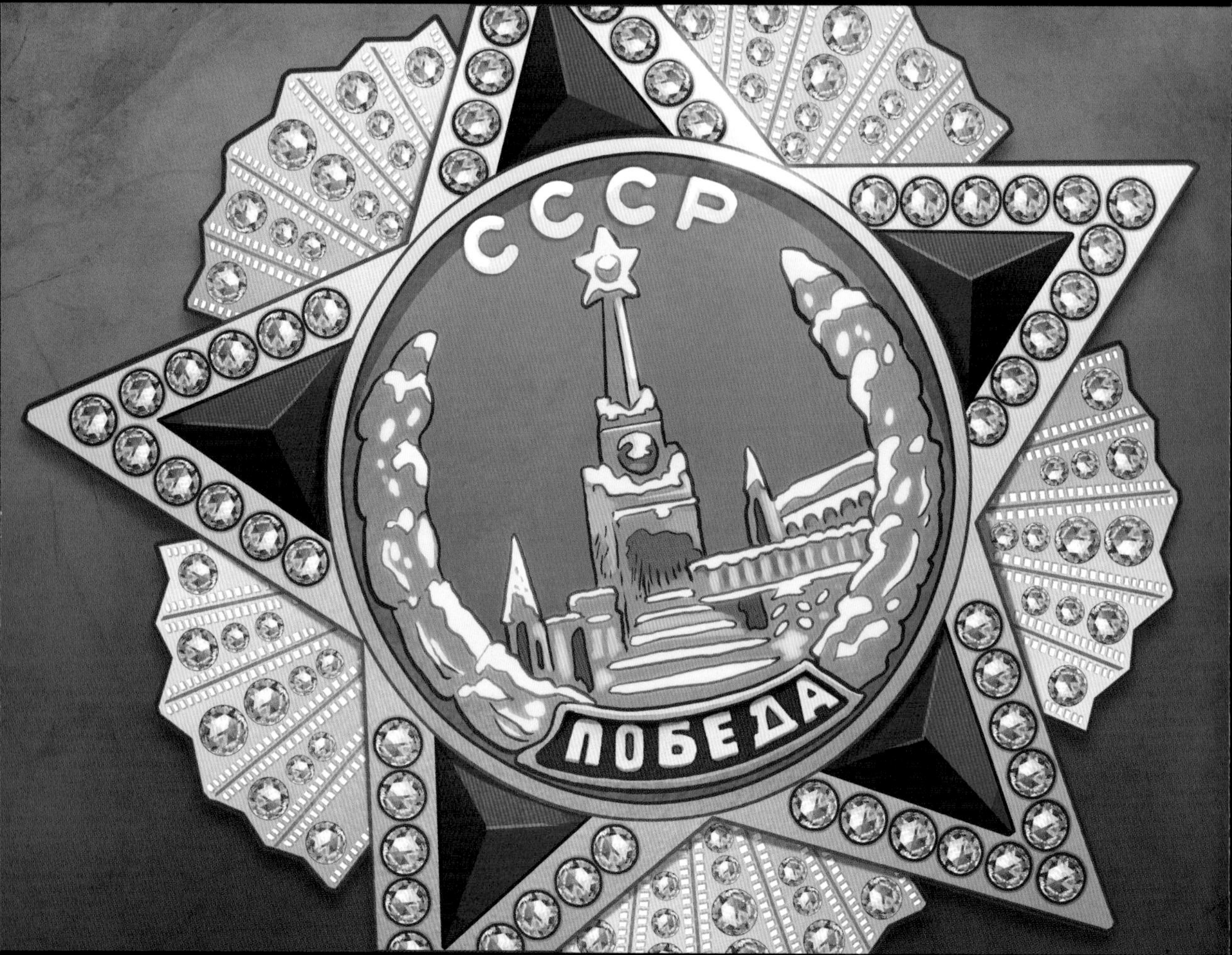
СССР
ПОБЕДА

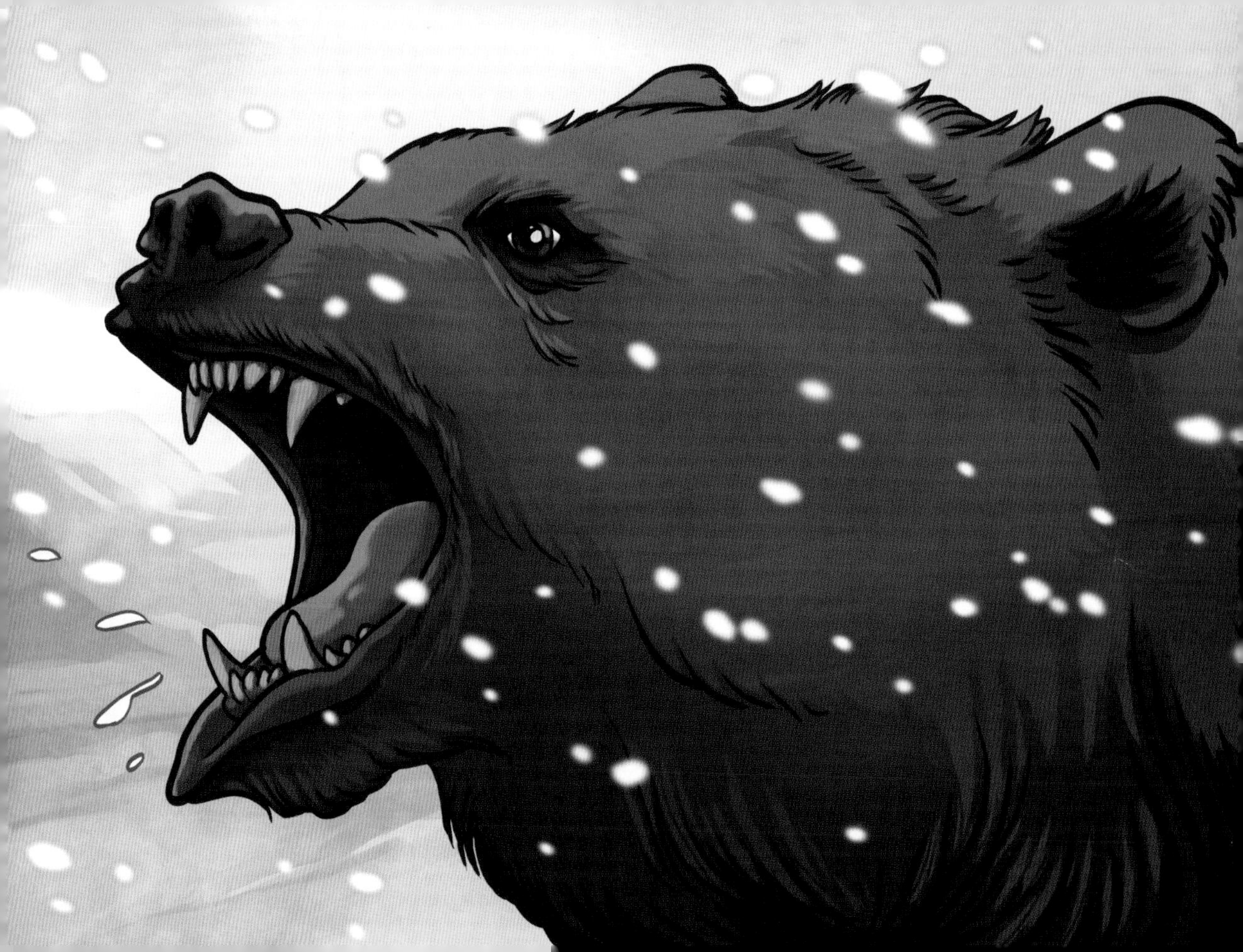

SCOTT PILGRIM:
PRECIOUS LITTLE BOX SET
Bryan Lee O'Malley
digest, b&w, includes poster
ISBN 978-1-934964-57-6

SCOTT PILGRIM: SPECIAL EDITION
VOLUME 1, HARD COVER
Bryan Lee O'Malley
184 pages, hardcover, color
ISBN 978-1-62010-000-4

THE SIXTH GUN, VOLUME 1:
COLD DEAD FINGERS
Cullen Bunn, Brian Hurtt, Bill Crabtree
176 pages, trade paperback, color
ISBN 978-1-934964-60-6